THE GREAT
CHICKEN
COOKBOOK

INTRODUCED BY JUDITH FERGUSON

PHOTOGRAPHY BY PETER BARRY

DESIGNED BY CLAIRE LEIGHTON AND RICHARD HAWKE

EDITED BY KATE CRANSHAW

TYPESETTING BY JULIE SMITH AND IMAGE SETTING

Recipes on pages 28, 32, 36, 42, 44, 48, 50, 52, 54, 60, 62, 92, 94, 114, 124, 126, 128, 130, 134, 138, 142, 158, 160, 164, 166 and 172, courtesy of the British Chicken Information Service

CLB 3255
© 1993 CLB Publishing

This edition published in 1995 by SMITHMARK Publishers, Inc.
16 East 32nd Street, New York NY 10016

SMITHMARK books are available for bulk purchase for sales promotion and premium use.
For details write or call the manager of special sales, SMITHMARK Publishers, Inc.
16 East 32nd Street, New York, NY 10016; (212) 532-6600

Produced by CLB Publishing, Godalming Business Centre, Woolsack Way, Godalming, Surrey, UK

ISBN 0-8317-4093-0

Printed in Singapore
10 9 8 7 6 5 4 3 2 1

THE GREAT

CHICKEN
COOKBOOK

JUDITH FERGUSON

SMITHMARK

CONTENTS

*I*NTRODUCTION

D own through the ages, politicians on both sides of the Atlantic have been promising a chicken in every pot. That's because chicken has always been a symbol of prosperity. Most countries in the world have a classic chicken dish in their culinary repertoire. In the USA it's Southern Fried Chicken, in France it's Coq au Vin, Hungary has Chicken Paprika, and Britain has its roast chicken with all the trimmings. In China and India the variations are too numerous to name just one.

Before the days of intensive farming, chickens were a once-a-week treat on Sunday, but as they became more readily available, problems developed. Chickens began to lose their flavor, and health hazards, due to the very techniques that made chicken more available, made people wary of eating them. This was a blessing in disguise, because it led the poultry industry to explore new ways of rearing chickens. As a result many birds were better fed and cared for, and the public was rewarded with birds with a much better flavor.

With the advent of new rearing ideas came corn-fed and free-range chickens. Corn-fed chickens have a golden color which is due to their feed, but they aren't necessarily free-range. Free-range chickens often have their diets supplemented with corn, so they, too, will have the same golden color.

There are other distinctions among chickens, too, as you will see, but whatever the description, chicken can be the basis for so many different, delicious and nutritious recipe ideas that you will never be lost for inspiration.

Types and cuts of chicken

Clockwise from top left: Oak-smoked chicken, corn-fed chicken, roasting chicken, chicken quarter, skinned chicken breast, chicken wing, chicken drumstick, chicken breast with skin, poussin, spatchcocked chicken.

Choosing Chicken

Poussin is the French name for young or "spring" chicken. Single poussins usually weigh about 14 ounces and serve one person; double poussins, weighing 1¼-1½ pounds, usually feed two people. Both can be fried, broiled or sautéed, and are often boned and stuffed, or spatchcocked (split and flattened out).

Broilers or roasting chickens can weigh anything from 2 to 6 pounds, the average being about 4½ pounds; and besides roasting, other cooking methods – such as frying, baking, or casseroling – work equally well.

A capon is a neutered young rooster. This process can be carried out by a small operation or by implanting hormones into the bird's neck. Capons are raised to be very plump, and can weigh up to 8 pounds. They are best roasted or casseroled to make the most of their rich and distinctive flavor.

Boiling or stewing chickens were once abundant, but are now seldom seen. These are older and tougher birds which need long, moist cooking and make delicious soups. A male chicken too old to roast is called a cock. A fowl is a hen of the same age.

Buying Chicken

You can buy chicken in many different forms – split in half, in quarters, portioned into thighs, drumsticks, wings or breasts. Breasts come bone-in, part-boned or completely boneless, with the skin on or off. Boned and skinned chicken breasts, which include the top bone of the wing, are called suprêmes. Chicken can be diced, ground, cut in strips for stir-frying, or threaded on skewers. You can choose from stuffed breasts, thighs or a whole stuffed bird ready for roasting. You will find chicken portions marinated, or in sauces ready to cook.

Chicken wrapped for the supermarket cabinet will be labeled with the date that it should be sold by, and the date that you should eat it by. Even through the wrapping, you can tell if a bird has bruised or otherwise damaged skin, by discolored patches or the skin looking shriveled and dry – all signs of a substandard bird. Where color is concerned, remember that battery-farmed chickens will look very pale compared to corn-fed or free-range ones. On chicken pieces, the flesh next to the bone is normally slightly darker. Most of the cuts that are available fresh, are also available frozen.

Storing Fresh and Frozen Chicken

If you can't take the chicken straight home from the supermarket or if the weather is very warm, take a insulated bag along with you to the store. Put the chicken into the refrigerat immediately or when you get it home, but not right next to cooked food or on the shelf above. Place the chicken in its wrapper on a plate large enough to contain any drips.

Don't freeze uncooked chicken unless you are certain it hasn't been frozen before. Never freeze chicken that isn't absolutely fresh. Any bacteria will just lie dormant while the chicken is frozen, and will start multiplying as soon as the chicken starts to thaw. If you buy it ready frozen, put it into your home freezer as soon as possible in its original wrapping. Freeze uncooked chicken for up to three months and cooked for up to two months, but check the manufacturers instructions for your freezer.

Whenever possible, thaw the chicken in the refrigerator or at least in a cool room. Make sure it is completely defrosted before cooking. There should be no ice crystals in the cavity, and the legs should be soft and flexible. There is really no nutritional difference between fresh and frozen chicken, providing it hasn't been frozen longer than the recommended time.

Nutritious Chicken

Chicken is a favorite with calorie – and health-conscious people for several very good reasons. It's low in fat, and contains a high proportion of unsaturated fatty acids, which is very important in low cholesterol diets. Although the skin contains the most calories, even with it, 3½ ounces of chicken is just 230 calories. Ounce for ounce chicken has more protein than red meat, and contains useful amounts of thiamine, riboflavin and nicotinic acid from the Vitamin B complex. The fact that it can be cooked so many different ways helps make low-fat or low-calorie diets more satisfying, too.

Preparing Chicken

There are a few commonsense rules to follow when preparing chicken:

Wash your hands thoroughly in hot, soapy water and rinse well.

Remove the chicken from the refrigerator just before you want to prepare it, so that it doesn't stand too long at room temperature.

Place chicken on a clean chopping board. Use one board for raw meat and poultry only. Plastic boards are more hygienic than wood as they can be more thoroughly cleaned after use.

Rinse chicken after cutting into pieces or before cooking it whole and pat dry on paper towels.

Cooking Chicken

Oven roasting
Cook a 3½ -pound chicken for 20 minutes per pound plus 20 minutes more at 375°F. Cook larger chickens at 325°F for about 25 minutes per pound, plus 25 minutes more.

For fast roasting set the oven to 400°F, cover the chicken completely with foil and roast for 20 minutes per pound plus 20 minutes more. Remove foil 20 minutes before the end of cooking time.

To test, stick a skewer into the thickest part of the thigh; if the juices run clear, the chicken is done.

Cook boned, stuffed chickens at 350°F for 30 minutes per pound, covered loosely. Test with a meat thermometer, in the center of the bird – it should read 170°F. Let sit for 10 minutes before removing the twine and carving.

Poaching

Rub the surface of a whole chicken with lemon juice, and place in a large pan with a bouquet garni (parsley stalk, bay leaf and sprig of thyme), a peeled carrot, a stalk of celery, an onion stuck with a clove, and enough water to cover. Bring to a boil, and skim any scum from the surface as it rises. Simmer, over a low heat until tender, about 2-3 hours. Cook uncovered for a clearer cooking liquid.

Strain and reserve the liquid. Let sit until the fat rises to the surface, then skim off or refrigerate overnight. The fat will solidify, and can then be easily lifted off the top of the liquid.

Chicken breasts can be poached in a skillet with stock and wine to cover, and seasoned with herbs. Simmer for 15-20 minutes, or until tender.

Stock making

Place raw or cooked bones in a large pan, and cover with water. Add a bouquet garni, chopped onion, carrot, celery, and a few black peppercorns. Add onion skin too, for a richer-looking stock. Seeded tomatoes can be added, and so can any root vegetable. Add giblets, if wished, but not the liver as this will make the stock bitter.

Bring to a boil, skimming off any scum that surfaces. Simmer for 2-3 hours, skimming occasionally. Strain and remove the fat in the same way as for poached chicken.

Stuffing a chicken

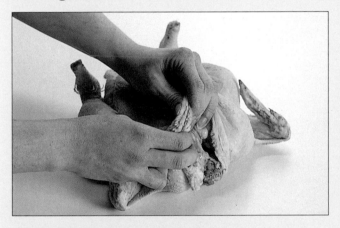

1 *Lift the neck flap and loosen the skin from the flesh around the wishbone.*

2 *Place the stuffing under the neck flap, pushing in as much as you can without stretching the skin too much.*

3 *Pull the neck flap back over the stuffing, shaping it until nicely rounded and plump. Tuck the ends under the wing tips, and secure with a skewer.*

An alternative way of stuffing is to loosen all the skin over the breast, and push the stuffing in between the flesh and the skin to cover the whole breast evenly.

Trussing a chicken

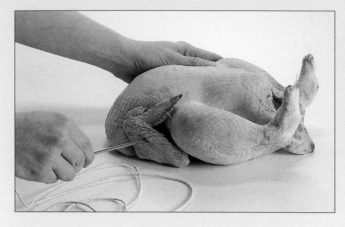

1 *Place chicken breast-side up, pass the trussing needle (threaded with twine) through one wing joint, leaving about 3 inches of string protruding from the wing, through the body of the chicken and out through the wing on the opposite side.*

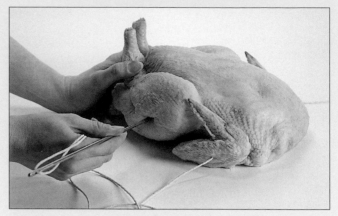

2 *Now push the needle through the skin just under the drumstick joint, through the body to come out in the same position on the opposite side.*

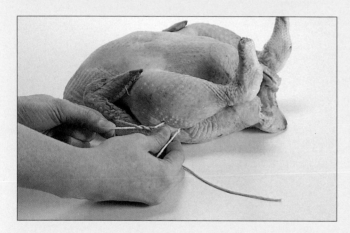

3 *Remove the needle, and tie the two ends of twine together securely.*

4 *Pass a piece of string under the "parson's nose," cross the string over, and bring one end under each leg.*

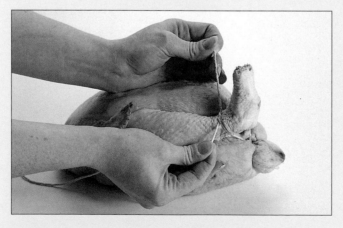

5 *Cross the ends over, back up across the legs and tie securely.*

Dividing a chicken

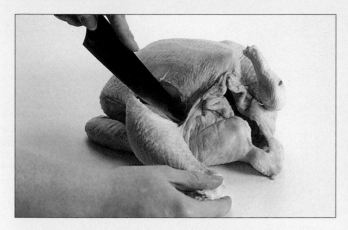

1 *Cut through the chicken at the point where each leg joins the body.*

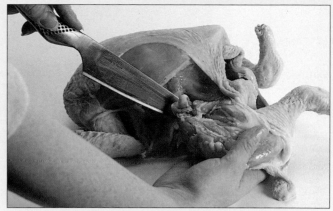

2 *Bend each leg outwards to break the ball and socket joint. Use the tip of a sharp knife to separate the oyster (succulent eye of meat) from underneath the body to detach each leg totally.*

3 *Turn the chicken upside down and using a sharp heavy knife or a pair of poultry shears, cut through both sides of the rib cage just underneath the breast meat and the wing joints.*

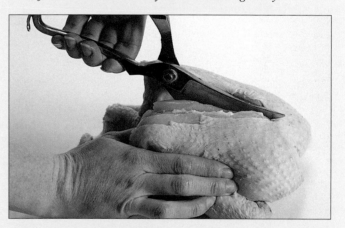

4 *Turn the chicken over again and cut all the way along the breast bone to divide it into two pieces.*

5 *Cut each breast piece into two, leaving a portion of white meat attached to the wing joints.*

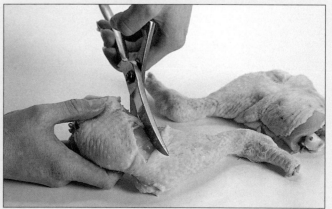

6 *Bend the leg pieces back and forth to find the joint between the drumstick and thigh, and cut between the two to separate them.*

Boning a whole chicken

1 *Place the chicken breast-side down on a chopping board, and using a sharp knife, cut through the skin along the backbone right down to the bone. Remove the "parson's nose."*

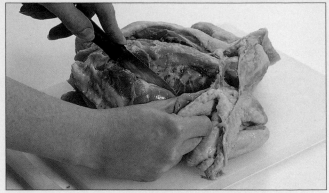

2 *Using the tip of a small sharp knife, scrape against the bone down the length of the cut you have made to begin lifting the skin and flesh away from the bone. Insure you do not cut through the skin, and always angle the knife into the bone.*

3 *Work the knife in the same way all the way down around the rib cage to the wing joints and leg joints.*

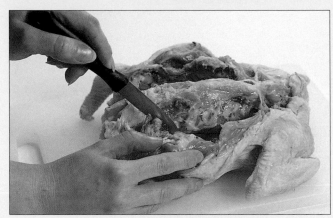

4 *Use the point of the knife to cut between the ball and socket joint of the leg. Sever the sinews to separate the legs from the body. Cut through the wing joints on both sides, and sever the sinews.*

5 *Continue cutting against the bones around the rib cage until you reach the breast bone. Cut around the wishbone, and remove it.*

6 *Starting at the neck end, cut close to the breast bone toward the tail end to remove the carcass. Lift the carcass as you cut, being careful not to nick the breast skin.*

Flattening and filling chicken breasts

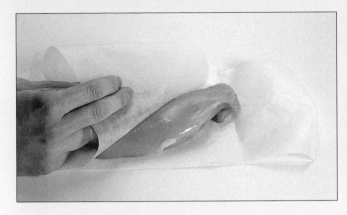

1 *Place the skinned chicken breast between two sheets of dampened baking parchment or waxed paper.*

2 *Use a rolling pin or meat mallet to flatten the chicken by beating it evenly from the middle out to the ends until it is about ⅓ inch thick.*

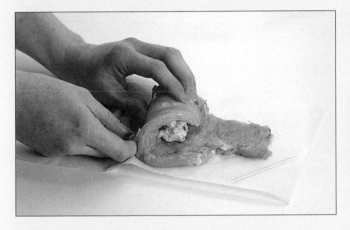

3 *Place filling on one end and fold in the sides to enclose. Roll up like a jelly roll, and secure with a toothpick.*

4 *Dust lightly with flour, brush with beaten egg, and then roll in bread crumbs. Deep-fry, shallow-fry or bake.*

Stuffing chicken breasts

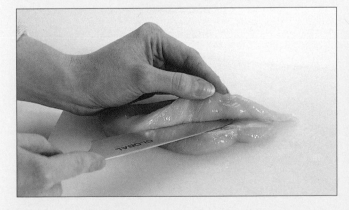

1 *On the thick side of the breast, cut a pocket along the side about ¼-½ inch from either end.*

2 *Fill with stuffing and reshape, securing the cut side with a skewer or toothpick.*

Braising, casseroling and sautéing

To braise, lightly brown a whole chicken or pieces in a little oil or butter, then remove and fry the chopped vegetables. Replace chicken on top, cover and cook at 325°F until tender.

To casserole, coat chicken pieces lightly in flour, then fry until golden. Add stock and wine to come nearly halfway up the chicken. Add chopped herbs, salt and pepper. Cover and cook for about 1 hour, as for braising. Add lightly cooked vegetables halfway through cooking.

To sauté, brown chicken pieces or halved poussins skin-side down in hot oil, or butter. Pour off most of the oil, and add the sauce ingredients to the pan. Cover and cook on the stove top until tender (about 30-40 minutes including browning time).

Stir-frying

For stir-frying, slice the chicken when it is very cold, because this makes it easier to handle, and allows thinner, more even strips to be cut. Use skinned and boneless breasts or thigh meat, and cut the meat into diagonal strips across the grain (this keeps the meat tender as it cooks), or into large dice.

Cook strips of chicken in a little oil in a wok or skillet over high heat. Keep the chicken moving as it cooks by tossing it with a spatula or large spoon. When almost cooked, add the other ingredients. Be sure to have everything prepared before starting to cook.

Broiling and frying

Use a spatchcocked bird or pieces; small chickens or poussins are the best size for this method of preparation.

Place the chicken breast-side down on a chopping board. Using poultry shears, cut down both sides of the back bone to remove it.

Turn the bird over, and press down very firmly on the breast bone with the heel of your hand until it cracks and the bird flattens out. Turn the drumsticks inward, and trim off the wing tips.

To make the bird easier to handle whilst cooking, and to help hold its shape, thread two long skewers diagonally through the bird from legs to opposite wings.

Marinate first, or just brush with oil and seasonings. Preheat the broiler, and cook about 10-15 minutes per side about 4 inches away from the heat.

For outdoor barbecuing, start grilling about 6 inches away from the coals, then move closer, or precook chicken, and then finish on the grill.

For frying, coat chicken portions in flour or with flour, then egg and finish with bread crumbs. For shallow frying, brown portions quickly in hot oil, then lower the heat and fry gently until the meat is tender – about 15-20 minutes. For deep-frying, choose pieces from a small chicken. Heat the oil to 375°F, and cook pieces for 10-15 minutes, turning frequently. Do not pierce the chicken when frying.

Roasting chicken

1 *Place the chicken in a roasting pan, and cover with foil.*

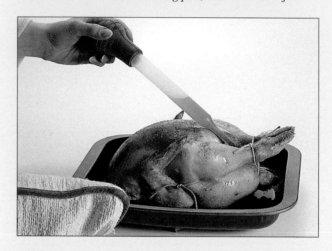

2 *Baste the chicken with the juices from the pan using a "bulb" baster.*

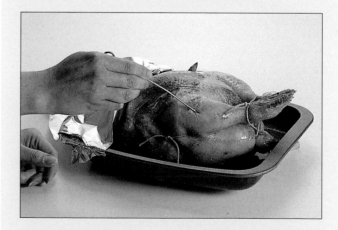

3 *To test the chicken to see if it is cooked, insert a skewer into the thickest part of the leg. If the juices run clear, the chicken is cooked; if the juices are pink, return the chicken to the oven for 10 minutes longer before testing again.*

Carving a cooked chicken

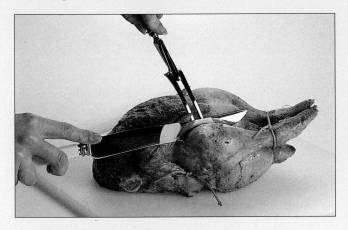

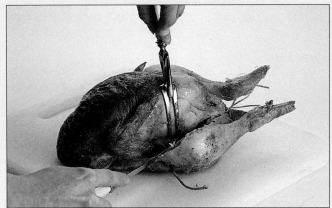

1 *Holding the chicken steady with a long pronged fork, cut down between the leg and body.*

2 *Break the joint by pressing one way with the carving knife and the opposite direction with the fork.*

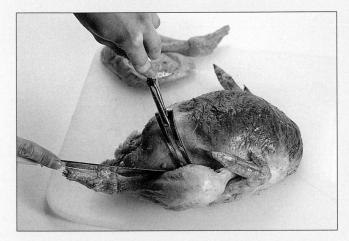

3 *Cut through the joint, keeping the "oyster" attached. Repeat this procedure with the other leg.*

4 *Use poultry shears or a heavy knife to sever the wing joints.*

5 *Holding the chicken firmly with the fork, carve the breast into slices with a sharp knife, cutting vertically from the top of the chicken parallel with the breast bone.*

Stock making

1 *Place raw or cooked chicken bones and giblets, minus the liver, in a large saucepan, and cover with water. Add a bouquet garni, some onion, celery, carrot and a few black peppercorns.*

2 *Bring to a boil, then reduce the heat and simmer for 2-3 hours. Skim off the scum from the surface.*

3 *Pour the finished stock through a fine strainer, and remove the fat before using.*

For goujons, cut skinned and boneless chicken breasts into thin strips lengthwise, sprinkle with seasoned flour and toss to coat evenly. This is easiest carried out in a plastic bag. Dip each strip into beaten egg, place some bread crumbs in a plastic bag and add a few egg-coated strips at a time, holding the bag closed and shaking it to coat the strips.

Cook goujons for about 3-5 minutes, turning often. Drain well on paper towels.

Microwaving
Brush the skin with basting mixtures containing soy sauce, Worcestershire sauce or paprika to make it look brown.

If your microwave manufacturer allows the use of foil, put a strip over the breast or on the leg and wing ends about halfway through cooking to prevent those parts overcooking.

Arrange chicken breasts in one layer in a round microwave dish with the thickest side to the outside of the dish.

Add a little liquid, but no salt as this can make the chicken tough and dry. Cover loosely to speed up cooking and keep the chicken moist. Cook on medium setting to prevent bursting. Turn the chicken over halfway through cooking.

Alternatively, brush breasts or thighs with oil, and coat in dry, seasoned bread crumbs. Place on a microwave rack to cook.

Always let microwaved chicken sit a few minutes after cooking.

Chicken can be successfully defrosted in a microwave oven. Cover it loosely, and turn over during defrosting. Always allow sitting time between defrosting and cooking, and follow your oven manufacturer's instructions.

Pressure cooking
Calculate cooking time from weight, including stuffing, if used. Pressure cookers cook in about a third of the time of conventional methods.

Chicken bricks
Soak the brick in water for 15 minutes each time before using it. Place the chicken in it, and start cooking on the lowest oven setting, increasing the heat every 5 minutes until the temperature reaches the required setting in your recipe.

Alternatively, set temperature at 350°F, and preheat the brick for 5 minutes, then put the chicken into it. Raise the oven temperature as the recipe requires, and bake the chicken.

Roasting bags
These keep the oven clean, and brown chickens very well while keeping them moist. Remember to make a few slits

in the bag to prevent it from exploding. A little flour added to the bag can help with self-basting.

Stuffings for Chicken

(for a 3½ pound chicken or 4 poussins)

BASIC BREAD STUFFING

2 tablespoons melted butter or margarine
1 small onion, finely chopped
3 cups fresh bread crumbs
Salt and pepper
2 teaspoons chopped herbs
1 egg, beaten
Stock or water

Melt butter or margarine, and cook the onion until softened. Combine with remaining ingredients, adding enough stock or water to bind the mixture.
Variations:
Cook 2 stalks chopped celery and/or 1⅓ cups sliced mushrooms with the onion.
Add 1 apple, cored and chopped, ⅓ cup golden raisins and ½ cup chopped walnuts.
Cook 8 ounces sausage meat, and add to the basic stuffing or with any variation, or add 6 cooked bacon slices, diced and cooked, or 1¼ cups chopped cooked ham.

CHESTNUT STUFFING

8 bacon slices, chopped
1 small onion, chopped
2 tablespoons butter
2 cups fresh breadcrumbs
1½-2 cups canned unsweetened chestnut purée, softened
1 tablespoon chopped parsley
Salt and pepper
1 egg, beaten

Fry bacon and onion in the butter until bacon is crisp. Combine with remaining ingredients, adding just enough egg to bind the mixture.

BASIC RICE STUFFING

2 tablespoons butter or margarine
1 small onion, chopped
⅔ cup long-grain rice
1¼ cups stock or water
1 tablespoon chopped herbs

Melt butter or margarine, and cook the onion until softened. Add the rice, and cook for 2-3 minutes. Pour on stock or water, and bring to a boil. Cover and simmer until the liquid is absorbed and rice is tender.

Variations:
Cook 2 stalks of chopped celery and 1⅓ cups sliced mushrooms with the onion and rice. Use ½ the onion and add 1 cup seedless, sliced grapes or 1 cup chopped, dried apricots and ½ cup toasted almonds. Use ⅓ cup wild rice combined with ⅓ cup brown or white rice.

SPICY CRACKED WHEAT STUFFING

¾ cup bulgar wheat
2 tablespoons olive oil
½ cup chopped almonds
4 scallions, chopped
½ teaspoon ground coriander
½ teaspoon ground cumin
Pinch of cayenne pepper
⅓ cup raisins
Salt
1 egg, beaten

Pour boiling water over the bulgar wheat to cover. Let it soak and absorb most of the water. Heat oil, and cook the almonds until pale golden. Add the onions and spices, and cook for about 1 minute. Combine with the drained bulgar and remaining ingredients, using only enough egg to bind.

Stuffing Boned Chicken

When stuffing a boned chicken (see step-by-step illustrations for method of boning) allow about 3 cups of stuffing for a 3½-pound chicken (whole weight).

Hold the end of the thigh bone, and scrape down around the length of it until you get to the place where it joins the drumstick. Cut through the joint to sever the thigh bone, but leave the drumstick in place.

Push some of the stuffing well into the spaces left by the removal of the thigh bones, and spread the remainder over the chicken meat, mounding it in the center and spreading enough over the neck flap to make it look plump. Make sure you leave enough skin to fold back over. Fold the neck flap and some skin at the tail end, back over the stuffing, and bring the sides to the center to overlap slightly.

Use a trussing needle, threaded with fine twine, to sew up the edges with a running stitch. Do not pull the stitches too tight as the stuffing will burst out during cooking. Tie the ends of the twine firmly to secure, and turn the chicken over. Plump the chicken up to shape it like a whole chicken, tucking the wing tips under the bird and pushing the drumsticks into the breast.

Truss the bird (see illustrated step-by-step guide), or just tie the legs together. To carve a cooked bird, simply cut off the wings and legs, then slice the body crosswise into thin slices. See **Oven roasting** section for cooking times.

CHAPTER 1

APPETIZERS
&
PARTY SNACKS

SERVES 4

CHICKEN SATAY

This typical Indonesian dish is very spicy,
and it makes an excellent appetizer for four.

2 tablespoons soy sauce
2 tablespoons sesame oil
2 tablespoons lime juice
1 teaspoon ground cumin
1 teaspoon ground turmeric
2 teaspoons ground coriander
1 pound chicken breast, cut into 1-inch cubes
2 tablespoons peanut oil
1 small onion, very finely chopped
1 teaspoon chili powder
½ cup crunchy peanut butter
1 teaspoon brown sugar
Lime wedges and fresh cilantro leaves, for garnish

1. Put the soy sauce, sesame oil, lime juice, cumin, turmeric and coriander into a large bowl, and mix well.

2. Add the cubed chicken to the soy sauce marinade, and stir well to coat the meat evenly.

3. Cover and chill for at least 1 hour, but preferably overnight.

4. Drain the meat, reserving the marinade.

5. Thread the meat onto 4 large or 8 small skewers, and set aside.

6. Heat the peanut oil in a small saucepan, and add the onion and chili powder. Cook over a low heat until the onion is slightly softened.

7. Stir the reserved marinade into the oil and onion mixture, along with the peanut butter and brown sugar. Cook over a low heat, stirring constantly, until all the ingredients are well blended. If the sauce is too thick, stir in 2-4 tablespoons boiling water.

Step 5 Thread the marinated meat onto 4 large, or 8 small, kebab skewers.

Step 9 Brush the partially broiled chicken with a little of the peanut sauce to baste.

8. Arrange the skewers of meat on the rack of a broiler pan, and cook under a preheated moderate broiler for 10-15 minutes. After the first 5 minutes of cooking, brush the skewered meat with a little of the peanut sauce to baste.

9. During the cooking time turn the meat frequently to cook it on all sides and prevent it browning.

10. Serve the skewered meat garnished with the lime and cilantro leaves, and pass the remaining sauce separately.

Cook's Notes

Time
Preparation takes about 25 minutes plus at least 1 hour marinating time, cooking takes about 15 minutes.

Serving Idea
Serve with a mixed salad.

SERVES 6-8

TERRINE OF SPINACH AND CHICKEN

This superb terrine is ideal when you want to impress
your guests with a delicious appetizer.

8 ounces boned and skinned chicken breasts
2 egg whites
2 cups fresh white bread crumbs
1 pound fresh spinach, washed
1 tablespoon each of finely chopped fresh chervil,
    chives and tarragon
Salt and freshly ground black pepper
1¼ cups heavy cream
½ cup finely chopped walnuts
Pinch nutmeg

Step 2 The
spinach should be
cooked until it is
just wilted, using
only the water that
clings to the leaves
and adding no
extra liquid.

1. Cut the chicken into small pieces, then put with 1 egg white and half of the bread crumbs into a food processor, and blend until well mixed.

2. Put the spinach into a large saucepan, and cover with a tight-fitting lid. Cook for 3 minutes, or until the spinach has just wilted.

3. Remove the chicken mixture from the food processor, and rinse the bowl. Put in the spinach, along with the herbs, remaining egg white and bread crumbs, and blend until smooth.

4. Season the chicken mixture with salt and pepper, and add half of the cream. Mix well to blend thoroughly. Add the remaining cream to the spinach, along with the walnuts and the nutmeg. Beat this mixture well to blend thoroughly.

5. Line an 8-by-4 inch loaf pan with baking parchment. Lightly oil this with a little vegetable oil. Pour the chicken mixture into the bottom of the pan, and spread evenly.

6. Carefully pour the spinach mixture over the chicken mixture, and smooth the top with a palette knife. Cover the pan with lightly oiled foil, and seal this tightly around the edges.

7. Stand the pan in a roasting dish, and pour enough warm water into the dish to come halfway up the sides of the pan. Cook in a preheated 325°F oven for 1 hour, or until it is firm.

8. Cool the terrine, then chill for at least 12 hours. Carefully lift the terrine out of the pans and peel off the parchment. To serve, cut the terrine into thin slices with a sharp knife.

Cook's Notes

 Time
Preparation takes 25
minutes, cooking takes
1 hour.

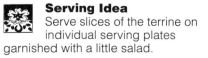 **Serving Idea**
Serve slices of the terrine on
individual serving plates
garnished with a little salad.

 Watchpoint
Do not overcook the terrine, or
attempt to cook it any more
quickly than the recipe states,
otherwise it will curdle and spoil.

SERVES 6

CHICKEN STUFFED BELL PEPPERS

Try a stuffing that is different from the
usual meat and rice one for light tasting peppers.

3 large green or red bell peppers
¼ cup butter or margarine
1 small onion, finely chopped
1 stalk celery, finely chopped
1 clove garlic, crushed
3 chicken breasts, skinned, boned and diced
2 teaspoons chopped fresh parsley
Salt and freshly ground black pepper
½ loaf of stale bread, made into crumbs
1-2 eggs, beaten
½ cup dry bread crumbs

1. Cut the bell pepper in half lengthwise, and remove the cores and seeds. Leave the stems attached, if wished.

2. Melt the butter in a skillet, and add the onion, celery, garlic and chicken. Cook over moderate heat until the vegetables are softened and the chicken is cooked. Add the parsley. Season with salt and pepper.

3. Stir in the dry bread-crumbs, and add enough beaten egg to make the mixture hold together.

4. Spoon filling into each bell pepper half, mounding the top slightly. Place the bell peppers in a baking dish that holds them closely.

5. Pour enough water down the inside of the dish to come about ½ inch up the sides of the peppers. Cover and bake in a preheated 350°F oven for about 45 minutes, or until the bell peppers are just tender.

6. Sprinkle each with the dry bread crumbs, and place under a preheated broiler until golden-brown.

Step 1 Cut bell peppers in half, and remove seeds and white core.

Step 4 Spoon filling into the bell pepper halves, mounding the top and smoothing out.

Step 5 Place bell peppers close together in a baking dish, and carefully pour in about ½ inch of water.

Cook's Notes

Time
Preparation takes about 30 minutes, cooking takes about 45-50 minutes.

Variations
Use scallions in place of the small onion. Add chopped nuts or black olives to the filling, if wished.

Serving Idea
Serve as a first course, either hot or cold, or as a light lunch with a salad.

SERVES 4

CHICKEN LIVER PÂTÉ

Deceptively quick and easy to prepare, this
creamy pâté is sure to be a firm favorite.

2 tablespoons butter, for frying
1 clove garlic, crushed
1 onion, finely chopped
Salt and freshly ground black pepper
8 ounces chicken livers, trimmed
1 teaspoon Worcestershire sauce
¼ cup butter, creamed
1 tablespoon brandy

Step 5 Add the creamed butter and brandy to the processed chicken livers, and blend until completely smooth.

Step 2 Increase the heat and sauté the chicken livers in the hot butter and onions for about 2 minutes, stirring until they are just cooked through.

1. Melt the butter in a skillet, and add the garlic, onion, salt and pepper. Sauté gently, until the onions have softened, but not colored.

2. Increase the heat, and stir in the chicken livers. Sauté for about 2 minutes on each side, stirring continuously, until just cooked through.

3. Add the Worcestershire sauce and stir.

4. Put the contents of the skillet into a food processor, or liquidizer, and blend for ½-1 minute until just smooth.

5. Add the creamed butter and the brandy to the processor, and process again until the pâté is smooth.

6. Transfer the pâté to 1 large dish, or 4 individual serving dishes, and chill until required.

Cook's Notes

 Time
Preparation takes about 15 minutes, cooking takes 15 minutes.

Preparation
If you do not have a liquidizer or food processor, the cooked chicken livers can be pressed through a wire strainer, using the back of a spoon, into a bowl; then beat in the butter and brandy to achieve the creamed pâté mixture.

 Cook's Tip
This pâté can be prepared ahead, but if you are not eating it straightaway, seal the surface with clarified butter, and chill until required.

SERVES 4

ORANGE AND CARDAMOM CHICKEN WINGS

The rather mysterious, perfumed flavor of cardamom is intriguing enough to use without many other ingredients, and almost everyone likes it.

8 chicken wings
4 cloves garlic, crushed
Finely grated rind 1 large orange
6 tablespoons orange juice
1 tablespoon lemon juice
4 tablespoons oil
Seeds from 10 cardamom pods, crushed
Salt and freshly ground black pepper

1. Wipe the chicken wings with paper towels. Cut off and discard the tips. Put the wings into a shallow ovenproof dish.

2. Mix the remaining ingredients together, pour over the chicken, and let marinate for at least 4 hours covered or up to 24 hours in the refrigerator.

3. Let the chicken come to room temperature, then cook uncovered in a preheated 400°F oven, for about 30 minutes, basting once or twice. Serve hot or cold.

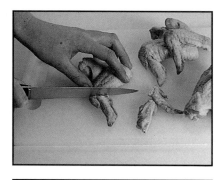

Step 1 Cut the tips off the chicken wings with a sharp knife.

Step 2 Mix all the ingredients together, and pour over the chicken, to marinate for at least 4 hours.

Cook's Notes

 Time
Preparation takes about 25 minutes, plus a minimum of 4 hours, marinating time. Cooking takes about 30 minutes.

 Serving Idea
Serve as a party snack or a picnic treat.

 Cook's Tip
The chicken wings should come to room temperature before cooking, otherwise they will take longer to cook.

SERVES 8

SESAME CHICKEN WINGS

This is an economical appetizer that is also good as a
cocktail snack or as a light meal with stir-fried vegetables.

12 chicken wings
1 tablespoon salted black beans
1 tablespoon boiling water
1 tablespoon oil
2 cloves garlic, crushed
2 slices fresh gingerroot, cut into fine shreds
3 tablespoons soy sauce
1½ tablespoons rice wine or dry sherry
Large pinch freshly ground black pepper
1 tablespoon sesame seeds

1. Cut off and discard the wing tips. Cut between the joint to separate into two pieces.

2. Crush the beans, and add the water. Let sit.

3. Heat the oil in a wok, and add the garlic and ginger. Stir briefly, and add the chicken wings. Cook, stirring, until lightly browned, for about 3 minutes. Add the soy sauce and wine, and cook, stirring, for about 30 seconds longer. Add the soaked black beans and pepper.

4. Cover the wok tightly, and let simmer for about 8-10 minutes. Uncover and turn the heat to high. Continue cooking, stirring until the liquid is almost evaporated and the chicken wings are glazed with sauce. Remove

Step 1 Use a knife or scissors to cut through thick joint, and separate the wing into two pieces.

Step 3 Fry garlic and ginger briefly, add the chicken wings, and cook, stirring, until lightly browned.

from the heat, and sprinkle on sesame seeds. Stir to coat completely and serve. Garnish with scallions or cilantro, if wished.

Cook's Notes

Time
Preparation takes about 25 minutes, cooking takes about 13-14 minutes.

Cook's Tip
You can prepare the chicken wings ahead of time, and reheat them. They are best reheated in the oven for about 10 minutes at 350°F.

Serving Idea
To garnish with scallion brushes, trim the roots and green tops of scallions and cut both ends into thin strips, leaving the middle intact. Place in iced water for several hours or overnight for the cut ends to curl up. Drain and use to garnish.

SERVES 4

Plum-Glazed Chicken Wings

This dish is extremely versatile. It can be cooked under the broiler,
in the oven or on the barbecue, and is delicious hot or cold.

8 chicken wings
½ onion, sliced
2-3 cloves garlic, chopped
1 bay leaf
2 star anise

Glaze
3 heaped tablespoons plum jam
1 teaspoon five-spice powder
1 tablespoons vinegar, cider or wine

Step 2 Mix together the plum jam, five spice powder and vinegar.

Step 1 Simmer the chicken wings in water with the onion, garlic, bay leaf, and star anise.

Step 3 Arrange the wings on the rack of a broiler pan, and brush with half the plum jam mixture.

1. Put the chicken wings in a saucepan with the onion, garlic, bay leaf and star anise. Cover with cold water, bring to a boil, and simmer for 10 minutes.

2. Mix together the jam, five-spice powder and vinegar, cider or wine.

3. Put the drained wings onto the rack of a broiler pan,

and brush with half the jam mixture. Broil under a high heat for 10 minutes, basting several times.

4. Turn the wings, brush with the remaining jam, and cook for 10 minutes longer until very brown, taking care not to burn the jam. Alternatively, the wings may be cooked in a preheated 425°F oven for 15 minutes, then for 15 minutes longer after the second coating of jam. Serve the wings hot or cold.

Cook's Notes

Time
Preparation takes about 10 minutes, cooking takes about 30 minutes.

Serving Idea
For a barbecue, a great accompaniment would be hot jacket potatoes with butter. Alternatively, serve on a bed of plain boiled rice.

Cook's Tip
If cooking these on a barbecue, be careful not to serve them immediately as the jam gets very hot and will easily burn unwary mouths.

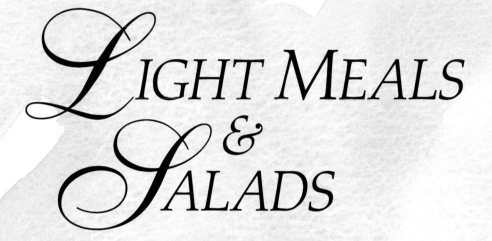

CHAPTER 2

LIGHT MEALS & SALADS

SERVES 4-8

CHINESE LEAF CHICKEN STIR-FRY SALAD

A more substantial version of the warm salad
which many restaurants serve as a first course.

4 tablespoons olive oil
3 cloves garlic, crushed
1 pound chicken breast, skinned and cut into
½-inch wide strips
3 cups shredded Chinese leaves
½ English cucumber, cut into 2-inch sticks
1 green bell pepper, cut into thin 2-inch strips
2 stalks celery, cut into thin 2-inch strips
1 tablespoon fresh parsley
2-3 tablespoons dry vermouth
Salt and freshly ground black pepper

1. Heat 3 tablespoons of the oil in a wok or skillet and
stir-fry the garlic and chicken over a medium high heat
for 10 minutes, or until tender and lightly browned but
cooked through. Remove the chicken, and keep warm.

2. Add the Chinese leaves, cucumber, bell pepper and

celery to the wok or skillet with the remaining oil, and
stir-fry for 2-3 minutes.

3. Turn the mixture onto a heated serving dish or
individual plates, then arrange the chicken on top.

4. Add the parsley and vermouth to the pan, and scrape
any browned pan juices from the bottom. Season, and
pour over the chicken and vegetables. Serve at once.

Step 2 Add the
Chinese leaves,
cucumber, bell
pepper and celery,
with the remaining
oil, and stir-fry for
2-3 minutes.

Step 1 Stir-fry the
garlic and chicken
strips over a
medium heat for
about 10 minutes,
or until lightly
browned and
cooked.

Step 4 Add the
parsley and
vermouth to the
pan, and scrape
up any browned
pan juices.

Cook's Notes

Time
Preparation takes about 5
minutes, cooking takes about
15 minutes.

Variation
Zucchini can be
substituted for the cucumber.

Serving Idea
Serve as a warm salad
for 6 or 8, or as an attractive
dinner or lunch for 4. It is essential to
serve this dish immediately, or the
fresh crunch of the green vegetables,
in contrast with the succulent chicken,
will be lost.

SERVES 4

CORONATION CHICKEN

This delicious, creamy dish is perfect fare
for that special summer picnic.

1¼ cups fromage frais or Quark
3-4 tablespoons mayonnaise
½-1 teaspoon curry paste (according to taste)
2 tablespoons apricot & ginger or mango chutney
3 cups diced cooked chicken
1 medium can apricot halves in natural juice, drained
Cup slivered almonds, toasted
Fresh parsley for garnish

Step 2 Add diced cooked chicken to the dressing.

Step 1 Mix fromage frais, mayonnaise, curry paste and chutney together well.

Step 3 Chop half the apricots, and add to the chicken.

1. Mix together the fromage frais, mayonnaise, curry paste and chutney in a large bowl until the curry is well blended. Taste and add more curry paste if required.

2. Add diced chicken meat.

3. Chop half of the apricots, and add to the mixture.

4. Pile onto a serving plate, and chill before serving. Garnish with the remaining apricots, sliced, and sprinkle with toasted almonds. Add some parsley sprigs if wished.

Cook's Notes

Time
Preparation takes 10-15 minutes plus chilling time.

Variation
Use canned mango or pineapple, instead of apricots.

Watchpoint
Do not add the toasted almonds until serving time, otherwise they will become soggy.

SERVES 4

TARRAGON CHICKEN PANCAKES

These attractive pancakes look sophisticated enough
for a dinner party, but are also so easy to make,
you can indulge yourself at any time.

1 cup whole wheat flour
1 egg
1¼ cups milk
Oil, for frying
⅓ cup all-purpose flour
1¼ cups milk
Salt and freshly ground black pepper
1½ cups cooked chicken, chopped
1 avocado, peeled, halved, pitted and chopped
2 teaspoons lemon juice
1 tablespoon chopped fresh tarragon

1. Put the whole wheat flour into a large bowl, and make a slight well in the center. Break the egg into the well, and begin to beat the egg carefully into the flour, incorporating only a little flour at a time.

2. Add the milk gradually to the egg and flour mixture, beating well between additions, until all the milk is incorporated and the batter is smooth.

3. Heat a little oil in a small skillet, or crêpe pan, and cook about 2 tablespoons of the batter at a time, tipping and rotating the pan, so that the batter spreads evenly over the base to form a pancake. Flip the pancake over, to cook the second side.

4. Repeat this process until all the batter has been used up. Keep the pancakes warm, until required.

5. Blend the all-purpose flour with a little of the milk, and gradually add the rest of the milk, until it is all incorporated.

6. Pour the flour and milk mixture into a small pan, and cook over a moderate heat, stirring continuously, until the sauce has thickened. Season to taste.

7. Stir the chopped chicken, avocado, lemon juice and tarragon into the sauce.

8. Fold each pancake in half, and then in half again, to form a triangle.

9. Carefully open part of the triangle out to form an envelope, and fill this with the chicken and avocado mixture.

Step 1 Put the flour into a bowl, and make a slight well in the center. Break the egg into this well, and beat gently, incorporating a little of the flour at a time.

Step 3 Using a small skillet, or crêpe pan, heat a little hot oil and fry 2 tablespoons of the batter at a time. Tip and rotate the pan while cooking, to distribute the batter evenly, and make a nice thin pancake.

Cook's Notes

 Time
Preparation takes about 25 minutes, cooking takes about 25 minutes.

 Preparation
Use 1¼ cups fromage frais, instead of the milk, for a luxurious change to this recipe.

 Serving Idea
Serve piping hot, garnished with watercress and a crisp green salad.

SERVES 4

CHICKEN SALAD WITH MANGO AND SOUR CREAM DRESSING

This recipe is a perfect way of turning leftover chicken into a delicious main course dish.

2 tablespoons chopped fresh chives, or 1 tablespoon dried chives
4 tablespoons dry white wine
⅓ cup good mayonnaise
⅓ cup sour cream
Scant 1 teaspoon powder mustard
Salt and freshly ground black pepper
1-2 mangoes, depending on size
1 pound cooked chicken breast, skinned and boneless

Step 2 Strain the chive mixture, pressing the chives to extract as much of their essence as possible.

Step 1 Simmer the chives and wine for 5 minutes, or until reduced to 1-2 tablespoons.

Step 5 Slice the chicken into roughly the same sized pieces as the mango.

1. Put the chives, with the wine, into a small pan, and simmer, uncovered, for about 5 minutes, until reduced to only 1 or 2 tablespoons.

2. Pour through a fine strainer, pushing the chives to extract as much of their essence as possible.

3. Mix the mayonnaise with the sour cream, mustard and about 1 tablespoon of the chive essence. Don't let the dressing become too thin, particularly if the dish is being made ahead.

4. Check the seasoning, adding salt and pepper if necessary.

5. Peel and slice the mango. Cut the cold chicken into slices of approximately the same size.

6. Arrange roughly in a shallow dish, and pour the dressing over, tossing lightly so that all the pieces are covered.

Cook's Notes

Time
Preparation takes about 25 minutes.

Serving Idea
This salad is delicious when served with a chilled Chardonnay wine.

Cook's Tip
If making this salad in advance, do not coat with the dressing until serving time.

SERVES 4

CURRIED CHICKEN DRUMSTICKS

This Tandoori recipe appeals to all age groups, and is perfect for barbecues or for informal parties as it can be made in large quantities.

8 chicken drumsticks
Juice of 2 lemons
4 large cloves garlic, crushed
1-inch piece fresh gingerroot, peeled and finely chopped
1 generous teaspoon ground cumin
2 teaspoons sweet paprika
2 teaspoons ground coriander
⅔ cup natural yogurt
¼ teaspoon chili powder or cayenne pepper

Step 2 Put the chicken into a shallow dish, and sprinkle with half the lemon juice.

Step 1 Dry the drumsticks, then score with a sharp knife.

1. Wipe the drumsticks with paper towels, and score with a sharp knife in several places.

2. Sprinkle with half the lemon juice, and put into a shallow dish. Mix the remaining ingredients together, and spread evenly over the chicken. Cover the dish, and let marinate overnight in the refrigerator.

3. Transfer the chicken to a foil-lined baking pan and cook, uncovered in a preheated 400°F oven for 30 minutes, turning halfway through.

4. Baste the chicken, and put under a hot broiler or on a barbecue for 10-15 minutes, turning and basting frequently until very brown.

Step 4 Transfer the chicken to a broiler pan, and baste with some of the marinade.

Cook's Notes

Time
Preparation takes about 15 minutes, plus overnight marinating time. Cooking takes about 40-45 minutes.

Variation
If liked, red food coloring may be added to the marinade for an authentic appearance, although this will not affect the flavor. For extra heat add more chili powder, or some mustard oil.

Serving Idea
Serve the chicken with lemon, cucumber, and a dressing of natural yogurt, into which you have stirred lots of chopped fresh mint.

SERVES 4

CHICKEN AND AVOCADO SALAD

The creamy herb dressing complements this easy summer salad.

8 anchovy fillets, soaked in milk, rinsed and dried
1 scallion, chopped
2 tablespoons chopped fresh tarragon
3 tablespoons chopped fresh chives
4 tablespoons chopped fresh parsley
1¼ cups prepared mayonnaise
⅔ cup natural yogurt
2 tablespoons tarragon vinegar
Pinch sugar and cayenne pepper
1 large head lettuce
1 pound cooked chicken
1 avocado, peeled and sliced or cubed
1 tablespoon lemon juice

1. Combine all the ingredients, except the lettuce, chicken, avocado and lemon juice, in a food processor. Work the ingredients until smooth, and well mixed. Chill for at least 1 hour for the flavors to blend.

2. Shred the lettuce or tear into bite-sized pieces, and arrange on plates.

3. Top the lettuce with the cooked chicken, cut into strips or cubes.

4. Spoon the dressing over the chicken. Brush the avocado slices, or toss the cubes, with lemon juice, and garnish the salad. serve any remaining dressing separately.

Step 1 The dressing should be very well blended after working in a food processor. Alternatively, use a hand blender.

Step 3 Arrange lettuce on individual plates, and top with shredded chicken.

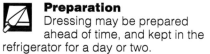
Cook's Notes

Time
Preparation takes about 30 minutes, plus 1 hour chilling.

Preparation
Dressing may be prepared ahead of time, and kept in the refrigerator for a day or two.

Serving Idea
The dressing may be served as a dip for vegetable crudités or with a tossed salad.

SERVES 4

APRICOT CHICKEN WITH MINT

This is a delicious recipe with a light, yogurt-based sauce of
the most beguilling pale apricot color and fascinating
clear flavor. It can be served hot or cold.

8 chicken thighs or drumsticks, skinned
½ cup finely chopped onion
1 orange
2 tablespoons lemon juice
½ cup dried apricots
2 tablespoons chopped fresh mint or 2 teaspoons
   dried mint
⅔ cup dry white wine
Salt and freshly ground black pepper
3-4 tablespoons thick natural yogurt, to serve

1. Put the chicken into a flameproof casserole, and add
the onion, finely grated rind of the orange with 4
tablespoons of juice, and the remaining ingredients
except the yogurt. Be generous with the mint, as much
of the flavor cooks away.

Step 1 Cover the
chicken with the
onion, orange rind
and juice, and add
the remaining
ingredients. Add
plenty of mint.

2. Cover and marinate for 2-4 hours or overnight, in the
refrigerator.

3. Let the chicken come to room temperature, then bake
covered, in a preheated 375°F oven for 45 minutes or
until tender. Remove the chicken and keep warm.

Step 4 Strain the
puréed sauce,
using the back of a
soup ladle for
speed, into a
saucepan.

4. Purée the rest of the casserole contents in a food
processor or liquidizer, and then force through a strainer
(using the back of a soup ladle for efficiency and speed)
into a saucepan.

5. Reheat but do not boil. Remove from the heat, and
stir in the yogurt, tasting all the time to get a pouring
sauce that is rich but light in flavor. Adjust the seasoning
with salt and pepper, and pour the sauce over the
chicken.

Cook's Notes

 Time
Preparation takes about 25
minutes, plus minimum of 2
hours, marinating time. Cooking
takes about 45 minutes.

Variation
You can serve this dish cold
for a buffet, in which case
you should cool the chicken and the
sauce separately.

 Serving Idea
You can serve the dish hot,
with the sauce in a separate
container as a dip. In both cases, it is
ideal with a mixed green salad.

SERVES 4

SAFFRON CHICKEN QUICHE

The exciting contrast of rich chicken and warm spices with the
sharpness of lemon and parsley is bridged by a sprinkle of sugar.

9-10 inch quiche pan, with pastry dough made with
   egg yolk
8 eggs
¼ cup butter
½ cup onion, finely chopped
6 tablespoons lemon juice
3 envelopes powdered saffron
12 ounces uncooked chicken meat, cut into long
   strips
2 teaspoons ground cinnamon
½ teaspoon white pepper
¼ cup fresh parsley, including stalks, coarsely
   chopped
1 teaspoon sugar

1. Line the pie shell with baking parchment, and cover
with baking beans (or use dried kidney beans, pasta or
rice). Put into a preheated 400°F oven and bake for 10
minutes. Remove the beans, carefully take off the baking
parchment, and return to the oven for 10 minutes longer
until the bottom is set.

2. Lightly beat a white from one of the eggs, and brush
this onto the hot pastry; return to the oven for a few
minutes to insure it sets and seals the pastry.

3. Melt the butter, add the onion, lemon juice and
saffron, and cook over a low heat until the onion is really
soft.

4. Stir in the chicken meat, cook over a low heat for 5
minutes, then set aside to cool.

5. Beat the cinnamon and white pepper into the eggs, and

Step 2 Paint the
hot pastry case
with the egg white
to seal it.

Step 3 Melt the
butter, add the
onion, lemon juice
and saffron, and
cook gently until
the onion is soft.

stir in the parsley and the juices from the cooked chicken.

6. Arrange the chicken neatly on the cooled pie shell,
and ladle on the egg mixture. Transfer to a preheated
325°F oven for 15 minutes.

7. Sprinkle with sugar, and return to the oven for 25
minutes longer, until lightly browned just around the
edges and only just set – it will firm up more once out
of the oven. (If you overcook the quiche, the eggs will
toughen.) Serve warm or cold.

Cook's Notes

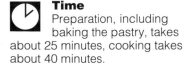 **Time**
Preparation, including
   baking the pastry, takes
about 25 minutes, cooking takes
about 40 minutes.

 Serving Idea
Serve warm or lightly chilled
at buffets or picnics, as either
a first or main course.

Variation
If you cannot find saffron but
like the yellow color, you can
substitute turmeric, but it will not give
quite the same flavor.

SERVES 4-6

LEFTOVER CHICKEN SALAD

This recipe is perfect for using up leftovers of cooked chicken.

2 ripe but firm avocados, or 1 mango
Lemon juice
4 tomatoes, peeled
1 pound cooked chicken meat, broken or cut into
   small cubes
2 scallions, chopped
2 tablespoons chopped fresh parsley
½ cup roasted cashew nuts
Fresh parsley to garnish

For the Garlic Vinaigrette
3 tablespoons groundnut oil
1 tablespoon white wine vinegar
1 teaspoon French mustard
1 clove garlic, crushed
½ teaspoon superfine sugar
Salt and freshly ground black pepper

1. Split the avocado in half, remove the pit and skin, and cut the flesh into neat slices. Brush with lemon juice to prevent discoloration. If using mango instead, peel and cut the flesh into neat slices.

2. Slice the tomatoes, and arrange alternately with the avocado or mango around the outer edge of a flat serving dish.

3. Mix the chicken with the scallions, parsley and nuts.

4. Whisk together the garlic vinaigrette ingredients, and use enough to coat the chicken well. Pile the mixture in the center of the avocado or mango and tomato.

5. Brush the avocado or mango and tomato with a little dressing, and sprinkle everything lightly with chopped parsley.

Step 1 Brush the sliced avocado with lemon juice to prevent discoloration.

Step 3 Mix together the cooked chicken, scallions, parsley and nuts.

Step 4 Pour enough vinaigrette over the chicken to coat it well.

Cook's Notes

 Time
Preparation takes about 25 minutes.

 Variation
Use pa payas, kiwi fruit or peaches in place of the avocado.

 Serving Idea
Serve the salad with whole wheat bread and butter and a chilled dry white wine.

SERVES 4

HERBY LEMON CHICKEN

Served either hot or cold, this refreshing recipe
is perfect for picnics and light suppers.

3 cups fresh white bread crumbs
2 tablespoons chopped fresh parsley
2 tablespoons chopped fresh tarragon
Zest 1 lemon
Salt and freshly ground black pepper
1 tablespoon Dijon mustard
¼ cup butter
8 chicken drumsticks, skinned
Flour for dusting
1 small egg, beaten

For the lemon and herb butter
½ cup slightly salted butter
Zest ½ lemon
Squeeze lemon juice
2 tablespoons chopped fresh parsley
2 tablespoons chopped fresh tarragon

Step 1 Mix bread crumbs, parsley, tarragon and lemon zest together.

1. Put the bread crumbs in a large, shallow bowl, and add the parsley, tarragon and lemon zest. Season with salt and pepper, and mix well.

2. Put the mustard and butter together in a saucepan, and melt. Remove from the heat, and add the bread crumb mixture, stirring well to coat all the bread crumbs in butter. Let cool.

3. Coat each drumstick, one at a time, with flour. Dip, one at a time, in the beaten egg, and then roll in the bread crumbs, pressing the mixture on gently to give an even coating.

4. Lay the drumsticks on a rack over a roasting pan and bake in a preheated 400°F oven for 30-40 minutes, or until golden and crisp.

5. Meanwhile, thoroughly mix together all the lemon and herb butter ingredients. Place on a piece of baking parchment and pat into a cylinder using a knife. Roll up the butter inside the paper, and twist the ends to seal. Chill until firm. To serve, unwrap and slice into rounds to accompany the chicken.

Step 3 Dust each drumstick with flour.

Step 3 Coat with bread crumb mixture, pressing on gently to give an even coating.

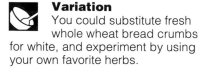

Cook's Notes

 **Time**
Preparation takes about 25 minutes, cooking takes about 30-40 minutes.

 Variation
You could substitute fresh whole wheat bread crumbs for white, and experiment by using your own favorite herbs.

Serving Idea
Serve hot with herb butter and a slice of lemon, or cold with a green salad.

SERVES 4

CHICKEN LIVERS WITH CHINESE LEAVES & ALMONDS

Chicken livers need quick cooking so are perfect for stir-frying.

8 ounces chicken livers
3 tablespoons oil
½ cup split blanched almonds
1 clove garlic, peeled
2 ounces snow peas
8-10 Chinese leaves, finely shredded
2 teaspoons cornstarch mixed with 1 tablespoon cold water
2 tablespoons soy sauce
⅔ cup chicken stock

Step 2 Cook the almonds slowly in the oil to brown evenly, stirring often.

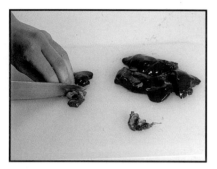

Step 1 Cut off any yellowish or greenish portions from the livers, and divide them into even-sized pieces.

Step 3 Quickly stir-fry the livers until lightly brown on the outside. May be served slightly pink in the middle.

1. Pick over the chicken livers and remove any discolored areas or bits of fat. Cut the chicken livers into even-sized pieces.

2. Heat a wok, and pour in the oil. When the oil is hot, turn the heat down, and add the almonds. Cook, stirring continuously, over a low heat until the almonds are a nice golden-brown. Remove and drain on paper towels.

3. Add the garlic, and cook for 1-2 minutes to flavor the oil, then remove. Add the chicken livers, and cook for

about 2-3 minutes, stirring frequently. Remove the chicken livers, and set them aside. Add the snow peas to the wok, and stir-fry for 1 minute. Add the Chinese leaves to the wok, and cook for 1 minute. Remove the vegetables, and set them aside.

4. Mix together the cornstarch and water with the soy sauce and stock. Pour into the wok, and bring to a boil. Cook until thickened and clear. Return all the other ingredients to the sauce, and reheat for 30 seconds. Serve immediately.

Cook's Notes

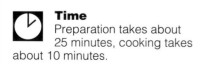
Time
Preparation takes about 25 minutes, cooking takes about 10 minutes.

Preparation
Remove any discolored portions from the livers as these can cause a bitter taste. Livers may be served slightly pink in the middle.

Serving Idea
Serve with plain or fried rice. Chinese noodles also make a good accompaniment.

SERVES 6

MEXICAN CHICKEN & BELL PEPPER SALAD

This is the perfect lunch or light supper dish during the summer.

1 pound cooked chicken, cut in strips
⅔ cup mayonnaise
⅔ cup natural yogurt
1 teaspoon chili powder
1 teaspoon paprika
Pinch cayenne pepper
½ teaspoon tomato paste
1 teaspoon onion paste
1 green bell pepper, finely sliced
1 red bell pepper, finely sliced
¾ cup frozen corn, defrosted
1¼ cups cooked long-grain rice, to serve

1. Place the chicken strips in a large salad bowl.

2. Mix the mayonnaise, yogurt, spices, tomato and onion purées together, and let sit briefly for flavors to blend. Fold dressing into the chicken.

3. Add the pepper and corn, and mix gently until all the ingredients are coated with dressing.

4. Place the rice on a serving dish, and pile the salad into the center. Serve immediately.

Step 3 Fold all ingredients together gently so that they do not break up. Use a large spoon or rubber spatula.

Step 4 Arrange rice on a serving plate, and spoon salad into the center.

Cook's Notes

Time
Preparation takes about 30 minutes.

Buying Guide
Onion paste is available in tubes like tomato paste.

Preparation
Chicken salad may be prepared several hours ahead and kept covered in the refrigerator. Spoon onto rice just before serving.

Variation
Add sliced green chilis or jalapeño peppers for hotter flavor. Try chili sauce or taco sauce as an alternative seasoning.

SERVES 4

MANGO CHICKEN THIGHS OR DRUMSTICKS WITH COCONUT

Slightly piquant and immensely satisfying and simple to make. Ideal cold in picnic hampers.

8 chicken thighs or drumsticks
½ cup mango chutney
⅓ cup shredded coconut
1 teaspoon mild curry paste
Lemon juice

1. Skin the chicken pieces, and with a sharp knife make a 1-inch slit along the bone.

2. Cut the flesh each side of the bone to make two small pockets, but don't cut all the way through.

3. Put the mango chutney into a strainer sitting over a bowl, and separate the solids from the sauce.

4. Chop the mango flesh roughly, mix with the coconut and curry paste, and add a squeeze of lemon juice.

5. Stuff the pockets with the mixture, and place them in a lightly oiled or greased baking dish.

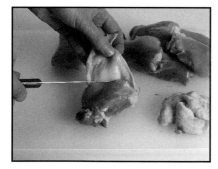

Step 1 Skin the chicken thighs or drumsticks with a sharp knife.

Step 5 Stuff the pockets with the mango mixture.

Step 6 Brush half the sauce over the chicken thighs before cooking.

6. Stir a squeeze of lemon juice into the reserved sauce from the mango chutney, and brush half of this over the thighs.

7. Bake uncovered in a preheated 400°F oven for 15 minutes, then brush with the remaining sauce and return to the oven for a further 15 minutes longer, or until cooked through and tender.

Cook's Notes

Time
Preparation takes about 15 minutes, cooking takes about 30 minutes.

Variation
This recipe can be varied by using peach chutney or any other chutney that has large, solid pieces of fruit in it.

Serving Idea
Choose the thighs if you are eating at a table, perhaps with a salad as either a first or main course. The drumsticks are ideal for picnics and buffets.

SERVES 4

SUMMER PICNIC PARMESAN AND HERB CHICKEN

This dish is fabulous served cold, when the flavors have had time
to mingle and develop. It is also good served warm – especially
in summer – with a chilled dry rosé wine from California.

½ cup grated Parmesan cheese
¼ cup ground almonds
4 tablespoons olive oil
4 cloves fresh garlic, or rather less if old
¼ cup fresh basil
3-pound roasting chicken
1 tablespoon extra Parmesan

4. Rub the extra Parmesan into the skin before putting
the bird into a roasting bag, or a roasting dish which you
can cover with a lid or foil.

5. Bake in a preheated 375°F oven for 20 minutes per
pound, plus 20 minutes extra.

Step 3 Press the
stuffing under the
skin, as evenly as
possible, to cover
the breast meat
and part of the
legs.

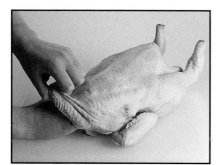

Step 2 Gently
ease the chicken
skin away from the
flesh, starting
around the
wishbone.

1. Mix together the cheese, almonds and oil to form a
soft paste. Finely slice the garlic, and chop the basil very
roughly. Stir these into the paste.

2. Gently ease the chicken skin away from the flesh,
starting around the wishbone.

3. Press the stuffing under the skin as evenly as you can,
covering the whole of the breast and some of the legs.
Pat the skin back over the bird.

Step 4 Rub the
extra Parmesan,
into the skin before
cooking.

Cook's Notes

 Time
Preparation takes about 25
minutes, cooking takes
about 1 hour 20 minutes.

 Serving Idea
Serve with a lovely, crisp,
green salad.

 Variation
Substitute any fresh herb such
as mint or parsley for the basil
– the dish will be equally delicious.

CHAPTER 3

FAMILY MAIN MEALS

SERVES 6

HONEY AND LEMON CHICKEN

Roast chicken is a firm favorite with everyone, and this
simple recipe is a delicious alternative to the traditional roast.

1 onion, finely chopped
½ cup wholewheat bread crumbs
Grated rind and juice of 1 lemon
1 egg, beaten
Salt and freshly ground black pepper
1 x 3½ pound roasting chicken
2 tablespoons clear honey
Butter or margarine
Fresh parsley and lemon slices for garnish

Step 2 Stuff chicken at the neck end.

Step 1 Combine onion, bread crumbs, half the lemon rind and juice, and egg for the stuffing.

Step 3 Brush well with honey and lemon juice 30 minutes before the end of cooking time.

1. Make a stuffing mixture by combining the finely chopped onion, bread crumbs, half of the lemon rind and juice, and the beaten egg, adding salt and pepper to taste.

2. Stuff the chicken at the neck end, then brush with a little melted butter or margarine. Cover with foil, and cook in a preheated 350°F oven for 20 minutes per pound, plus 20 minutes extra.

3. Thirty minutes before the end of cooking, take the chicken out of the oven, remove the foil, and brush liberally with a mixture of the clear honey and remaining lemon juice. Return to the oven until chicken is cooked and golden. Serve garnished with parsley and lemon slices.

Cook's Notes

 Time
Preparation takes about 15 minutes, cooking takes about 1 hour 40 minutes.

 Serving Idea
Serve as a traditional roast or enjoy cold, when the lemon flavor really comes through.

 Cook's Tip
When calculating the cooking time, remember to use the stuffed weight of the chicken.

SERVES 4-6

CHICKEN AND SAUSAGE RISOTTO

This is really a one-pot meal and one
you won't have to cook in the oven.

3 pounds chicken pieces, skinned, boned, and cut
  into cubes
4½ cups water
3 tablespoons butter or margarine
1 large onion, roughly chopped
3 stalks celery, roughly chopped
1 large green bell pepper, roughly chopped
1 clove garlic, crushed
Salt and freshly ground black pepper
1⅓ cups uncooked rice
14 ounce can tomatoes
6 ounces smoked sausage, cut into ½-inch dice
Chopped fresh parsley

1. Use the chicken skin and bones, onion and celery
trimmings to make stock. Cover ingredients with the
water, bring to a boil, and simmer slowly for 1 hour.
Strain and reserve.

2. Melt the butter or margarine in a large saucepan, and
add the onion. Cook slowly to brown. Then add the
celery, green bell pepper and garlic, and cook briefly.

3. Add salt and pepper and the rice, stirring to mix well.

4. Add the chicken, tomatoes, sausage and 1 quart of
the stock, and mix well. Bring to a boil, reduce the heat
to simmering, and cook for about 20-25 minutes, stirring
occasionally until the chicken is done and the rice is
tender. The rice should have absorbed most of the liquid
by the time it has cooked. Garnish with chopped parsley.

Remove the skin
from the chicken,
and set aside.

Step 1 Put the
skin and bones in a
large pot with the
onion and celery
trimmings to make
the stock. Add
water to cover.

Cook's Notes

Time
Preparation takes about
35-40 minutes, cooking takes
about 20-25 minutes.

Preparation
Check the level of liquid
occasionally as the rice is
cooking, and add more water or stock
as necessary. If there is a lot of liquid
left and the rice is nearly cooked,
uncover the pan and boil rapidly.

Serving Idea
Accompany with a green salad
to make a complete meal.

SERVES 6

CHICKEN COBBLER

This dish is warming winter fare with its
creamy sauce and tender, light topping.

2 chicken breasts and 2 chicken legs
6 cups water
1 bay leaf
4 whole peppercorns
2 carrots, peeled and diced
24 pearl onions, peeled
⅓ cup frozen corn
⅓ cup heavy cream
Salt and freshly ground black pepper

Cobbler Topping
3½ cups all-purpose flour
1½ tablespoons baking powder
Pinch salt
Scant ⅓ cup butter or margarine
Approximately 1½ cups milk
1 egg, beaten with a pinch of salt

1. Place the chicken in a deep saucepan with the water,
bay leaf and peppercorns. Cover and bring to a boil.
Reduce the heat, and let simmer for 20-30 minutes, or
until the chicken is tender. Remove the chicken from the
pot, and let cool. Skim and discard the fat from the
surface of the stock, Skin the chicken, and remove the
meat from the bones.

2. Continue to simmer the stock until reduced by about
half. Strain the stock, and add the carrots and onions.
Cook until tender, and add the corn. Stir in the cream,
add the chicken and season. Pour into a casserole or
into individual baking dishes.

3. To prepare the topping, sift the dry ingredients into
a bowl, or place them in a food processor and process
once or twice to sift.

4. Rub in the butter or margarine until the mixture
resembles bread crumbs. Stir in enough of the milk until
the mixture comes together.

5. Turn out onto a floured surface, and knead lightly.
Roll out with a floured rolling pin to about ½ inch
thickness, and cut with a 2-inch cooky cutter. Brush the
surface of each round with a mixture of egg and salt.
Place the rounds on top of the chicken mixture, and
bake in a preheated 375°F oven for 10-15 minutes.
Serve immediately.

Step 4 Rub the
butter or margarine
into the dry
ingredients until
the mixture
resembles bread
crumbs.

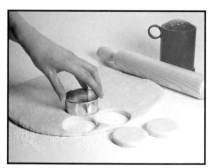

Step 5 Roll out
the mixture on a
floured surface, cut
into rounds, and
place on top of the
chicken mixture.

Cook's Notes

 Time
Preparation takes about 25
minutes, cooking takes 20-30
minutes for the chicken, about 20
minutes to prepare the sauce, and
10-15 minutes to finish off the dish.

 Preparation
When the topping has been
prepared, it must be baked
immediately, or the baking powder
will stop working and the cobbler
topping will not rise.

 Variations
Diced potatoes and pimento
may be added to the sauce
along with other vegetables. Add
chopped fresh parsley or a pinch of
dried thyme as well, if wished.

SERVES 4

FRIED CHICKEN

Fried Chicken is easy to prepare and when it's
homemade, it's much better than a take-out!

3 pounds chicken pieces
2 eggs
2 cups all-purpose flour
1 teaspoon each salt, paprika and sage
½ teaspoon black pepper
Pinch cayenne pepper (optional)
Oil for frying
Fresh parsley or watercress

Step 4 Coat the chicken on all sides with flour, shaking off the excess.

Step 2 Dip the chicken pieces in the egg to coat them well.

Step 6 Fry the chicken skin-side first for 12 minutes, turn over, and fry for 12 minutes longer.

1. Rinse chicken and pat dry with paper towels.

2 Beat the eggs in a large bowl, and add the chicken one piece at a time, turning to coat.

3. Mix flour and seasonings in a large plastic bag.

4. Place chicken pieces coated with egg into the bag, one at a time, close bag tightly, and shake to coat each piece of chicken. Alternatively, dip each coated chicken piece in a bowl of seasoned flour, shaking off the excess.

5. Heat oil in a large skillet to the depth of about ½ inch.

6. When the oil is hot, add the chicken skin-side down first. Fry for about 12 minutes, and then turn over. Fry for 12 minutes longer or until the juices run clear.

7. Drain the chicken on paper towels, and serve immediately. Garnish the serving plate with parsley or watercress.

Cook's Notes

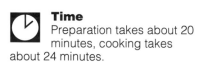 **Time**
Preparation takes about 20 minutes, cooking takes about 24 minutes.

Preparation
The chicken should not be crowded in the skillet. If your skillet is small, fry the chicken in several batches.

 Cook's Tip
When coating anything for frying, be sure to coat it just before cooking. If left to sit, coating will usually become very soggy.

SERVES 4

CHICKEN ESCALOPES

There are a multitude of different methods of cooking
chicken, and this one, although one of the simplest,
is also one of the most delicious.

4 boned and skinned chicken breasts
1 egg white
½ cup whole wheat bread crumbs
1 tablespoon chopped fresh sage
Salt and freshly ground black pepper
2 tablespoons walnut oil
½ cup mayonnaise
⅓ cup natural unset yogurt
1 teaspoon grated fresh horseradish
2 tablespoons chopped walnuts
Lemon slices and chopped walnuts to garnish

1. Pat the chicken breasts dry with paper towels.

2. Beat the egg white with a fork until it just begins to
froth, but is still liquid.

3. Carefully brush all surfaces of the chicken breasts
with the beaten egg white.

4. Put the bread crumbs onto a shallow plate, and mix
in the chopped sage. Season with salt and freshly
ground black pepper.

5. Place the chicken breasts, one at a time, onto the
plate of bread crumbs and sage, and carefully press
this mixture onto the surfaces of the chicken.

6. Put the oil into a large skillet, and cook the prepared
chicken breasts over a low heat on each side for 6-8
minutes until they are lightly golden and tender. Set
them aside, and keep warm.

7. Mix all the remaining ingredients, except for the
garnish, in a small bowl, whisking well to blend the
yogurt and mayonnaise evenly.

8. Place the cooked chicken breasts on a serving dish,
and spoon a little of the sauce over. Serve garnished
with lemon slices and additional chopped walnuts.

Step 2 Beat the
egg white with a
fork until it
becomes frothy,
but still liquid.

Step 5 Press the
bread crumb and
sage mixture onto
all surfaces of the
chicken breasts,
making sure that
they are covered
evenly.

Cook's Notes

Time
Preparation takes about
20 minutes, cooking takes
12-16 minutes.

Variation
Use almonds instead of
walnuts in this recipe, and
limes instead of lemons. Oranges
and hazelnuts make another
delicious variation.

Serving Idea
Serve with lightly cooked
thin green beans and new
potatoes, or rice.

SERVES 6

COUNTRY CAPTAIN CHICKEN

A flavorful dish named after a sea captain
with a taste for the spicy cuisine of India.

3 pounds chicken pieces, skinned
Seasoned flour
6 tablespoons oil
1 medium onion, chopped
1 medium green bell pepper, chopped
1 clove garlic, crushed
Pinch salt and freshly ground black pepper
2 teaspoons curry powder
2 14-ounce cans tomatoes
2 teaspoons chopped fresh parsley
1 teaspoon chopped fresh marjoram
4 tablespoons currants or raisins
1 cup blanched almond halves

1. Dredge the chicken with flour, shaking off the excess.

2. Heat the oil in a large skillet, and brown the chicken on all sides until golden. Remove to an ovenproof casserole.

3. Pour off all but 2 tablespoons of the oil. Add the onion, bell pepper and garlic, and cook slowly to soften.

4. Add the seasoning and curry powder, and cook, stirring frequently, for 2 minutes. Add the tomatoes, parsley and marjoram, and bring to a boil. Pour the sauce over the chicken, cover and cook in a preheated 350°F oven for 45 minutes. Add the currants or raisins during the last 15 minutes.

5. Meanwhile, toast the almonds in the oven on a baking sheet along with the chicken. Stir them frequently, and watch carefully. Sprinkle over the chicken just before serving.

Step 4 Add the curry powder to the vegetables in the skillet, and cook for 2 minutes over a low heat stirring frequently.

Step 4 Cook the remaining sauce ingredients, and pour over the chicken.

Step 5 Toast the almonds on a baking sheet in the oven until light golden brown.

Cook's Notes

Time
Preparation takes about 30 minutes, cooking takes about 50 minutes.

Preparation
Country Captain Chicken can be prepared completely ahead, and reheated for about 20 minutes in a moderate oven.

Serving Idea
If wished, serve the chicken with an accompaniment of boiled rice.

SERVES 4

CHICKEN WITH "BURNED" BELL PEPPERS AND CILANTRO

"Burning" peppers is a technique for removing the skins
that also imparts a delicious flavor to this favorite vegetable.

2 red bell peppers, halved lengthwise and seeded
1 green bell pepper, halved lengthwise and seeded
4 tablespoons vegetable oil, for brushing
1 tablespoon olive oil
2 teaspoons paprika
¼ teaspoon ground cumin
Pinch cayenne pepper
2 cloves garlic, crushed
1 1-pound can tomatoes, drained and chopped
3 tablespoons chopped fresh cilantro
3 tablespoons chopped fresh parsley
Salt, for seasoning
4 large, boned chicken breasts
1 large onion, sliced
½ cup slivered almonds

1. Put the bell peppers, cut-side down, on a flat surface, and gently press them with the palm of your hand to flatten them out.

2. Brush the skin-side with 2 tablespoons of the vegetable oil and cook them under a hot broiler until the skin chars and splits.

3. Wrap the bell peppers in a dish cloth for 10 minutes to cool.

4. Unwrap the bell peppers' and carefully peel off the charred skin. Chop the flesh into thin strips.

5. Heat the olive oil in a skillet and gently fry the paprika, cumin, cayenne pepper and garlic for 2 minutes, stirring to prevent the garlic from browning.

6. Stir in the tomatoes, cilantro, and parsley, and season with a little salt. Simmer for 15-20 minutes, or until thick. Set aside.

7. Heat the remaining vegetable oil in a flameproof dish, and sauté the chicken breasts, turning them frequently until they are golden-brown on both sides.

8. Remove the chicken, and set aside. Gently fry the onion in the oil for about 5 minutes, or until softened but not overcooked.

9. Return the chicken to the casserole with the onion, and pour on about 1¼ cups of water. Bring to a boil.

10. Cover the casserole, and simmer for about 30 minutes, turning the chicken occasionally to prevent it from burning.

11. Remove the chicken from the casserole, and boil the remaining liquid rapidly to reduce to about ⅓ cup of stock.

12. Add the bell peppers and the tomato sauce to the chicken stock, and stir well.

13. Return the chicken to the casserole, cover and simmer very gently for 30 minutes longer, or until the chicken is tender.

14. Arrange the chicken on a serving dish with a little of the sauce spooned over. Sprinkle with slivered almonds, and serve any remaining sauce separately.

Cook's Notes

 Time
Preparation takes 30 minutes, cooking takes about 1 hour 30 minutes.

 Preparation
Take care not to cook this dish too rapidly, or the bell peppers will disintegrate.

SERVES 4

CHICKEN AND CASHEW NUTS

Many oriental dishes are stir-fried. This simply means that
they are fried quickly in hot oil, the ingredients being stirred
continuously to prevent them from burning.

12 ounces chicken breast, sliced into 1-inch pieces
1 tablespoon cornstarch
1 teaspoon salt
1 teaspoon sesame oil
1 tablespoon light soy sauce
½ teaspoon sugar
5 tablespoons vegetable oil
2 scallions, trimmed and chopped
1 small onion, diced
1-inch piece fresh gingerroot, peeled and finely
    sliced
2 cloves garlic, finely sliced
3 ounces snow peas
½ cup bamboo shoots, thinly sliced
1 cup cashew nuts
2 teaspoons cornstarch
1 tablespoon hoisin sauce, or barbecue sauce
Generous cup chicken stock

Step 2 Put the chicken pieces into the marinade mixture, and stir together well, to coat the pieces evenly.

Step 4 Add the mange tout and the bamboo shoots to the stir-fried onions in the wok, and continue stir-frying for about 3 minutes.

1. Roll the chicken pieces in the cornstarch. Reserve
any excess cornstarch.

2. Mix together the salt, sesame oil, soy sauce and sugar
in a large mixing bowl. Put the chicken into this marinade
mixture, and chill for 10 minutes.

3. Heat 2 tablespoons of the vegetable oil in a wok, and
stir-fry scallions, onion, ginger and garlic for 2-3 minutes.

4. Add the snow peas and the bamboo shoot to the
onion mixture. Stir-fry for 3 minutes longer.

5. Remove the fried vegetables. Add a further 1
tablespoon of oil to the wok, and heat through.

6. Lift the chicken pieces out of the marinade, and stir-

fry these in the hot oil for 3-4 minutes, until cooked
through.

7. Remove the cooked chicken pieces, and wipe the
wok clean.

8. Add the remaining oil, and return the chicken and
fried vegetables to the wok. Stir in the cashew nuts.

9. Mix together the 2 teaspoons of cornstarch, plus the
excess, with the hoisin or barbecue sauce and the
chicken stock. Pour this over the chicken and vegetables
in the wok, and cook over a moderate heat, stirring
continuously, until the ingredients are heated through
and the sauce has thickened.

Cook's Notes

Time
Preparation takes about
15 minutes, cooking takes
about 15 minutes.

Variation
Stir ¾ cup pineapple
chunks into the stir-fry
mixture just before serving.

Serving Idea
Serve this stir-fry with a dish of
Chinese noodles.

SERVES 4-6

LEMON CHICKEN

Chicken, lemon and basil is an ideal flavor combination,
and one that is used often in Greek cookery.

2 tablespoons olive oil
2 tablespoons butter or margarine
1 3-pound chicken, cut into 6-8 pieces
1 small onion, cut in thin strips
2 stalks celery, shredded
2 carrots, cut in julienne strips
1 tablespoon chopped fresh basil
1 bay leaf
Grated rind and juice of 2 small lemons
⅔ cup water
Salt and freshly ground black pepper
Pinch sugar (optional)
Lemon slices for garnishing

1. Heat the oil in a large skillet. Add the butter or margarine, and, when foaming, place the chicken, skin-side down, in one layer. Brown and turn over. Brown the other side. Cook the chicken in two batches if necessary. Remove the chicken to a plate, and set aside.

2. Add the vegetables, and cook 2-3 minutes over a moderate heat. Add the basil, bay leaf, lemon juice and rind, water, salt and pepper, and replace the chicken. Bring the mixture to a boil.

3. Cover the pan, and reduce the heat. Let simmer for about 35-45 minutes, or until the chicken is tender and the juices run clear when the thighs are pierced with a fork.

4. Remove the chicken and vegetables to a serving dish, and discard the bay leaf. The sauce should be

To cut the onion in thin strips, first cut in half through the root end. Using a sharp knife, follow the natural lines in the onion, and cut through neatly to the flat base. Cut off the root end, and the onion will fall apart in strips.

To make the carrots easier to cut into julienne strips, first cut them into rectangular blocks.

Cut the carrot blocks into thin slices, and then stack them up to cut into strips quickly.

thick, so boil to reduce if necessary. If the sauce is too tart, add a pinch of sugar. Spoon the sauce over the chicken to serve, and garnish with lemon slices.

Cook's Notes

Time
Preparation takes about 30 minutes, cooking takes about 45-55 minutes total, including browning of chicken.

Variation
Use limes instead of lemons and oregano instead of basil.

Serving Idea
Pasta that is often served with chicken dishes in Greece. Rice is also a good accompaniment, along with a green salad.

SERVES 4-6

CHICKEN WITH OLIVES

This is a chicken sauté dish for olive lovers.
Use more or less of them as your own taste dictates.

2 tablespoons olive oil
2 tablespoons butter or margarine
1 3-pound chicken, cut in 6-8 pieces
1 clove garlic, crushed
⅔ cup white wine
⅔ cup chicken stock
Salt and freshly ground black pepper
4 zucchini, cut in ½-inch pieces
20 pitted black and green olives
2 tablespoons chopped fresh parsley

1. Heat the oil in a large skillet and add the butter or margarine. When foaming, add the chicken skin-side down in one layer. Brown one side of the chicken, and turn over to brown the other side. Cook the chicken in two batches if necessary.

To peel a garlic clove easily, first crush it gently with the side of a large knife. The skin will split, making it easier to remove.

To cut the zucchini quickly into chunks, first top and tail them, then cut them in half if small, or quarters if large, lengthwise. Gather the strips together, and cut crosswise into chunks of the desired size.

Step 1 Cook the chicken, skin-side down first, until golden-brown.

2. Turn the chicken skin-side up, and add the garlic, wine, stock, salt and pepper. Bring to a boil, cover the pan, and simmer over a low heat for about 30-35 minutes.
3. Add the zucchinis and cook for 10 minutes. When the chicken and zucchinis are cooked, add the olives and cook to heat through. Add the parsley, and remove to a dish to serve.

Cook's Notes

Time
Preparation takes about 25 minutes, cooking takes about 50-55 minutes.

Serving Idea
Serve with rice or pasta and tomato salad.

Variation
Artichoke hearts may be used in place of the zucchini.

SERVES 4-6

CHICKEN CACCIATORE

The name means Chicken the Hunter's Way,
and that means the addition of mushrooms.

3 tablespoons oil
4 ounces mushrooms, quartered, if large
1 3-pound chicken, skinned if wished and cut into
 pieces
1 onion
2 cloves garlic
⅔ cup vermouth
1 tablespoon white wine vinegar
⅔ cup chicken stock
1 1-pound can tomatoes
1 teaspoon fresh oregano
1 sprig fresh rosemary
Salt and freshly ground black pepper
½ cup pitted black olives
2 tablespoons chopped fresh parsley

1. Hcat the oil in a heavy-bottomed skillet and cook the mushrooms for about 1-2 minutes. Remove them, and set aside. Brown the chicken in the oil, and transfer the browned pieces to an ovenproof casserole.

2. Chop the onion and garlic finely. Pour off all but 1 tablespoon of the oil in the skillet and reheat the pan. Cook the onion and garlic until softened but not colored. Add the vermouth and vinegar, and boil to reduce by half. Add the chicken stock, tomatoes, oregano, rosemary, salt and pepper. Break up the tomatoes and bring the sauce to a boil. Let cook for 2 minutes.

3. Pour the sauce over the chicken in the casserole, cover and cook in a preheated 350°F oven for about 1 hour.

4. Add mushrooms and olives during the last 5 minutes of cooking.

5. Remove the rosemary before serving, and sprinkle with chopped parsley.

Step 2 Cut onion in half lengthwise leaving the root end intact. Holding the knife parallel to the chopping board, cut the onion in thin horizontal slices, but not through to the root end.

Step 2 Cut the onion lengthwise in thin strips, leaving the onion attached at the root end.

Step 2 Cut crosswise through the onion; the onion will fall apart into small dice.

Cook's Notes

Time
Preparation takes about 25-30 minutes, cooking takes about 1 hour 15 minutes.

Cook's Tip
Pitted black olives are available in most good supermarkets and delis.

Serving Idea
Serve with spaghetti or pasta shapes, and sprinkle with grated Parmesan cheese.

COUNTRY CHICKEN STEW

SERVES 6-8

Bell peppers, potatoes, corn, tomatoes, onions and
fava beans are staple ingredients in this recipe.

3 pounds chicken pieces
⅓ cup all-purpose flour
3 tablespoons butter or margarine
8 ounces belly pork, rinded and cut into ¼-inch dice
3 medium onions, finely chopped
2 quarts water
3 14 ounce cans tomatoes
3 tablespoons tomato paste
1 cup fresh or frozen fava beans
½ cup corn
2 large red bell peppers, cut into small dice
3 medium potatoes, peeled and cut into ½-inch
  cubes
1-2 teaspoons cayenne pepper or Tabasco to taste
2 teaspoons Worcestershire sauce
1¼ cups red wine
Salt and freshly ground black pepper

1. Shake the pieces of chicken in the flour in a plastic bag to coat. In a large skillet, melt the butter until foaming. Place in the chicken, without crowding the pieces, and brown over a moderately high heat for about 10-12 minutes. Remove the chicken, and set it aside.

2. In the same skillet, fry the belly pork until the fat is rendered and the dice are crisp.

3. Add the onions, and cook over moderate heat for about 10 minutes, or until softened but not browned.

4. Pour the water into a large pot or saucepan, and spoon in the onions, pork and any meat juices from the skillet. Add the chicken, tomatoes and tomato paste. Bring to a boil, reduce the heat, and simmer for about 1-1½ hours.

5. Add the fava beans, corn, bell peppers and potatoes. Add cayenne pepper or Tabasco to taste. Add the Worcestershire sauce and red wine. Season to taste.

6. Cook for a further 30 minutes, or until the chicken is tender. Add salt and pepper to taste.

7. The stew should be rather thick, so if there is too much liquid, remove the chicken and vegetables, and boil down the liquid to reduce it. If there is not enough liquid, add more water or chicken stock.

Step 3 Add the onions, and cook slowly until tender but not browned.

Step 4 Scrape the contents of the skillet into a large pot or saucepan of water.

Cook's Notes

 Time
Preparation takes about 1 hour, cooking takes about 2 hours.

 Preparation
If wished, prepare the stew ahead, leaving out the last 30 minutes of cooking. Bring slowly to a boil, and then simmer for about 30 minutes longer before serving.

 Freezing
The stew may be frozen for up to 2 months in rigid containers. Cool the stew to room temperature before freezing.

SERVES 4

POULET FRICASSÉE

This is a white stew, enriched and thickened with an egg and cream mixture which is called a liaison in French cooking.

¼ cup butter
1 3-pound chicken, quartered and skinned
¼ cup all-purpose flour
2½ cups chicken stock
Grated rind and juice of ½ lemon
1 bouquet garni
12-16 small onions, peeled
12 ounces button mushrooms, whole if small, quartered if large
2 egg yolks
6 tablespoons heavy cream
3 tablespoons milk (optional)
Salt and freshly ground black pepper
2 tablespoons chopped fresh parsley and thyme
Lemon slices to garnish

1. Melt 3 tablespoons of the butter in a large skillet. Arrange the chicken in one layer, and cook over a low heat for about 5 minutes, or until the chicken is no longer pink. Do not let the chicken brown. If necessary, cook the chicken in two batches. When the chicken is sufficiently coked, remove it from the pan, and set aside.

2. Stir the flour into the butter remaining in the skillet, and cook over a very low heat, stirring continuously for about 1 minute, or until a pale straw color. Remove the pan from the heat, and gradually beat in the chicken stock. When blended smoothly, add lemon juice and rind, return the pan to the heat, and bring to a boil, whisking constantly. Reduce the heat, and let the sauce simmer for 1 minute.

3. Return the chicken to the skillet with any juices that have accumulated, and add the bouquet garni. The

Step 3 Tie a bay leaf, sprig of thyme and parsley stalks together to make a bouquet garni.

sauce should almost cover the chicken. If it does not, add more stock or water. Bring to a boil, cover the skillet and reduce the heat. Let the chicken simmer gently for 30 minutes.

4. Meanwhile, melt the remaining butter in a small skillet. Add the onions, cover and cook very gently for 10 minutes. Do not let the onions brown. Remove the onions from the skillet with a draining spoon, and add to the chicken. Cook the mushrooms in the remaining butter for 2 minutes. Set the mushrooms aside, and add them to the chicken 10 minutes before the end of cooking.

5. Test the chicken by piercing a thigh portion with a sharp knife. If the juices run clear, the chicken is cooked. Transfer the chicken and vegetables to a serving plate, and discard the bouquet garni. Skim the sauce of any fat, and boil it rapidly to reduce by almost half.

6. Blend the egg yolks and cream together, and whisk in several spoonfuls of the hot sauce. Return the egg yolk and cream mixture to the remaining sauce, and cook gently for 2-3 minutes. Stir the sauce constantly and do not let it boil. If very thick, add milk. Adjust the seasoning, stir in the parsley and thyme, and spoon over the chicken in a serving dish. Garnish with lemon slices.

Cook's Notes

 Time
Preparation takes about 30 minutes, cooking takes about 30-40 minutes.

 Serving Idea
Serve with boiled potatoes or rice.

 Cook's Tip
Pour boiling water over the onions, and let soak for 10 minutes to make them easier to peel.

 Watchpoint
A fricassée is a white stew. Cook gently to avoid browning the ingredients.

SERVES 4

SIMPLE CHICKEN CASSEROLE

This is really a cheat's recipe – a can of soup saves a
great deal of time, but the end result is delicious.

1 tablespoon oil
2 tablespoons butter
8 chicken thighs
1 10-ounce can condensed cream of mushroom soup
2½ cups sliced button mushrooms
3 tablespoons light cream
4 tablespoons dry sherry

1. Heat the oil and butter in a heavy-bottomed skillet. Add the chicken pieces skin-side down, and cook until golden-brown; then turn them, and brown the other side.

2. Mix the can of soup, the sliced mushrooms, cream and sherry together.

3. Place the chicken in an ovenproof dish or casserole, and pour the sauce over. Cover and bake in a preheated 375°F oven for 1¼-1½ hours, or until the chicken is tender.

Step 1 Sauté the chicken pieces on both sides until golden-brown.

Step 2 Mix the soup, mushrooms, cream and sherry together.

Cook's Notes

 Time
Preparation takes about 10 minutes, cooking takes about 1¼-1½ hours.

Variation
You can add shallots to the sauce for more flavor.

 Serving Idea
Serve with sautéed potatoes or rice and green beans.

SERVES 4

CHICKEN WITH CILANTRO AND PILAU RICE

Exotic spices used to be a frequent accompaniment to
chicken dishes, and this dish combines a wide selection of spices.

2 tablespoons oil
2 tablespoons butter
8 chicken thighs
1 large onion, sliced
1 teaspoon paprika
1 teaspoon cumin powder
1 teaspoon turmeric
½ teaspoon dried thyme
Freshly ground black pepper
1¼ cups well-flavored chicken stock
About 10 pitted black olives
2 tablespoons finely chopped fresh cilantro
Squeeze lemon juice

For the Pilau Rice
3 tablespoons butter
½ cup whole blanched almonds
1 small onion, finely diced
⅓ cup golden raisins or raisins
2 cups long-grain rice
2¾ cups boiling water
½ teaspoon salt

1. Heat the oil and butter in a large skillet and sauté the chicken until an even golden-brown color. Transfer to a plate.

2. Add the onion to the remaining fat, and sauté until softened and tinged with brown.

3. Add the paprika, cumin and turmeric, and cook for 1 minute. Add the thyme, black pepper and stock, and bring to a boil.

4. Return the chicken to the pan, skin-side down. Cover

and simmer for 40-45 minutes, or until tender.

5. Remove the chicken with a slotted spoon to a warm serving dish, and keep warm.

6. Reduce the sauce by boiling rapidly until it thickens. Stir in the olives, cilantro and lemon juice, season to taste and spoon over the chicken.

Step 6 Stir the olives, cilantro and lemon juice into the thickened sauce.

7. To prepare the pilau rice, melt 1 tablespoon of the butter in a small pan. When hot, add the almonds, and fry until lightly tinged with brown.

8. Dip the base of the pan into cold water to cool it down and prevent further cooking.

9. Melt the remaining butter in a large saucepan, and fry the onion over a low heat until softened, but not colored.

10. Add the fried almonds, golden raisins and rice, and fry for 1 minute. Add the boiling water and salt. Bring to a boil. Cover, reduce the heat to low and simmer for 15 minutes, until all the water has been absorbed.

11. Fork the rice lightly, and serve with the chicken.

Cook's Notes

Time
Preparation takes about 20 minutes, cooking takes 40-45 minutes.

Serving Idea
A chilled white wine made with German-Alsatian grapes complements this dish well.

Preparation
Prepare the pilau rice while the chicken is cooking, so they are both ready to serve at the same time.

SERVES 4

CHICKEN WITH SAFFRON RICE AND PEAS

Saffron gives rice and sauces a lovely golden color and delicate taste.

2 tablespoons oil
1 2¼-pound chicken, cut into 8 pieces and skinned if wished
Salt and freshly ground black pepper
1 small onion, finely chopped
2 teaspoons paprika
1 clove garlic, crushed
8 tomatoes, peeled, seeded and chopped
1¾ cups long grain rice
2¾ cups boiling water
Large pinch saffron or ¼ teaspoon ground saffron
1 cup frozen peas
2 tablespoons chopped fresh parsley

1. Heat the oil in a large skillet. Season the chicken with salt and pepper, and place it in the hot oil, skin-side down first. Cook over moderate heat, turning the chicken frequently to brown it lightly. Set the chicken aside.

2. Add the onions to the oil, and cook slowly until softened but not colored.

3. Add the paprika, and cook for about 2 minutes, stirring frequently until the paprika loses some of its red color. Add the garlic and the tomatoes.

4. Cook the mixture over high heat for about 5 minutes to evaporate the liquid from the tomatoes. The mixture should be of dropping consistency when done. Add the rice, water and saffron, and stir together.

5. Return the chicken to the casserole, and bring to a boil over a high heat. Reduce to simmering, cover tightly, and cook for about 20 minutes. Remove the chicken, and add the peas and parsley. Cook for 5-10 minutes longer, or until the rice is tender. Combine with the chicken to serve.

Step 3 Add the paprika, and cook until it loses some of its red color.

Step 4 When the garlic and tomatoes are added, cook over a high heat to evaporate the liquid until the mixture is of a dropping consistency.

Step 5 Stir in the peas and parsley, and cook for 5 minutes.

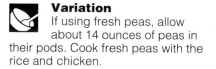

Cook's Notes

 Time
Preparation takes about 20-25 minutes, cooking takes about 25-35 minutes.

 Variation
If using fresh peas, allow about 14 ounces of peas in their pods. Cook fresh peas with the rice and chicken.

Serving Idea
This is a very casual, peasant-type dish which is traditionally served in the casserole in which it was cooked.

SERVES 4

POACHED CHICKEN WITH CREAM SAUCE

Plainly cooked chicken can be as flavorful as it is attractive.

1 4½-pound chicken
8-10 celery stalks, washed, cut into 3-inch lengths
   and tops reserved
6 thick slices bacon
2 cloves garlic, crushed
1 large onion, stuck with 4 cloves
1 bay leaf
1 sprig fresh thyme
Salt and freshly ground black pepper
Water to cover
⅓ cup butter or margarine
⅓ cup flour
1¼ cups light cream

1. Tie the chicken legs together, then place in a large casserole or pot. Chop the celery tops, and add to the pot. Place the bacon over the chicken, and add the garlic, onion with the cloves, bay leaf, sprig thyme, salt, pepper and water to cover.

2. Bring to a boil, reduce the heat and simmer gently, covered, for 50 minutes, or until the chicken is just tender. Add the celery, and simmer 20 minutes longer, or until the celery is just tender.

3. Remove the chicken to a serving plate, and keep warm. Strain the stock, and reserve the bacon and celery pieces. Skim fat off the top of the stock, and add enough water to make up 2½ cups, if necessary.

4. Melt 1 tablespoon of the butter or margarine in the casserole, and sauté the bacon until just crisp. Drain on paper towels and crumble roughly.

5. Melt the remaining butter in the casserole, and when foaming take off the heat. Stir in the flour, and gradually add the chicken stock. Bring to a boil, stirring constantly. Add the cream, and simmer until the mixture is thickened.

6. Untie the legs, and trim leg ends. If wished, remove the skin from the chicken before coating with the sauce. Garnish with the bacon and the reserved celery pieces.

Step 1 Tie the legs together, but do not cross them over.

Step 1 Arrange the bacon over the chicken, add the celery tops and the remaining ingredients.

Cook's Notes

Time
Preparation takes about 20 minutes, cooking takes about 1 hour 10 minutes.

Serving Idea
The chicken may be cut into 8 pieces before coating with sauce, if wished. Cut the leg joint in two, dividing the thigh and the drumstick. Cut the breast in two, leaving some white meat attached to the wings. Cut though any bones with scissors.

Variation
Sliced or whole baby carrots may be added with the celery. Small onions may also be cooked with the celery.

SERVES 6

TOMATO AND BACON FRIED CHICKEN

Not the usual crisp fried chicken, this is cooked in
a tomato sauce flavored with garlic, herbs and wine.

Flour for dredging
Salt and freshly ground black pepper
1 3-pound chicken, cut into serving pieces
6 tablespoons oil
Scant ⅓ cup butter or margarine
1 clove garlic, crushed
1 small onion, finely chopped
¾ cup diced bacon
6 tomatoes, peeled and chopped
2 teaspoons fresh thyme or 1 teaspoon dried thyme
⅔ cup white wine
2 tablespoons chopped fresh parsley

1. Mix the flour with salt and pepper and dredge the chicken lightly, shaking to remove any excess flour. Heat the oil in a large skillet, and, when hot, add the butter.

2. Add the chicken drumstick and thigh pieces skin-side down, and let brown. Turn the pieces over, and brown on the other side. Brown over moderately low heat, so that the chicken cooks as well as browns. Push the chicken to one side of the skillet, add the breast meat, and brown in the same way.

3. Add the garlic, onion and bacon to the skillet and lower the heat. Cook slowly for about 10 minutes, or until the bacon browns slightly. Add the tomatoes and thyme, and lower the heat. Cook until the chicken is just tender and the tomatoes are softened.

4. Using a draining spoon, transfer the chicken and other ingredients to a serving dish, and keep warm. Remove all but about 4 tablespoons of the fat from the pan, and deglaze with the wine, scraping up the browned bits from the bottom. Bring to a boil and let reduce slightly. Pour over the chicken to serve, and sprinkle with chopped parsley.

Step 1 Dredge the chicken very lightly with flour, and shake to remove the excess.

Step 2 Brown all the chicken on both sides slowly, until golden.

Cook's Notes

 Time
Preparation takes about 25 minutes, cooking takes, about 30-40 minutes.

Preparation
Brown the chicken slowly so that it cooks at the same time as it browns. This will cut down on the length of cooking time needed when all the ingredients are added.

 Variation
Add finely chopped green or red bell pepper or celery along with the onion and garlic. If more sauce is preferred, use one 14-ounce can of tomatoes and juice. Substitute chicken stock for the wine.

SERVES 6

CHICKEN WITH CLOUD EARS

Cloud ears is the delightful name for an edible tree
fungus which is mushroom-like in taste and texture.

12 cloud ears, wood ears or other dried Chinese
   mushrooms, soaked in boiling water for 10 minutes
1 pound skinned and boned chicken breasts, thinly sliced
1 egg white
2 teaspoons cornstarch
2 teaspoons white wine
2 teaspoons sesame oil
1¼ cups oil for deep-frying
1-inch piece fresh gingerroot, left whole
1 clove garlic
1¼ cups chicken stock
1 tablespoon cornstarch
3 tablespoons light soy sauce
Pinch salt and freshly ground black pepper

1. Soak the mushrooms until they soften and swell. Mix the chicken with the egg white, the 2 teaspoons cornstarch, the wine and sesame oil.

2. Heat the wok for a few minutes, and pour in the oil for deep-frying. Add the whole piece of ginger and whole garlic clove to the oil, and cook for about 1 minute. Remove them, and reduce the heat.

3. Add about a quarter of the chicken at a time, and stir-fry for about 1 minute. Remove and continue cooking until all the chicken is fried. Remove all but about 2 tablespoons of the oil from the wok.

4. Drain the mushrooms, and squeeze them to extract all the liquid. If using mushrooms with stems, remove the stems before slicing thinly. Cut cloud ears or wood ears into smaller pieces. Add to the wok, and cook for about 1 minute.

5. Add the stock, and let it come almost to a boil. Mix together the 1 tablespoon cornstarch and soy sauce, and add a spoonful of the hot stock. Add the mixture to the wok, stirring constantly, and bring to a boil. Let boil for 1-2 minutes, or until thickened. The sauce will clear when the cornstarch has cooked sufficiently.

6. Return the chicken to the wok, and add salt and pepper. Stir thoroughly for about 1 minute, and serve immediately.

Step 1 Soak the cloud ears or mushrooms in boiling water for 10 minutes; they will swell.

Step 3 Stir-fry the chicken in small batches, placing in the oil with chopsticks.

Cook's Notes

 Time
Preparation takes about 25 minutes, cooking takes about 5 minutes.

 Preparation
If wished, the chicken may be cut into 1-inch cubes. If slicing, cut across the grain as this helps the chicken to cook more evenly.

 Buying Guide
Dried cloud ears or wood ears are available from Chinese supermarkets and some delis. Shiitake mushrooms are more widely available. Both keep a long time in their dried state.

SERVES 4

CHICKEN POLISH-STYLE

Choose small, young chickens for a truly Polish-style dish. A dried white roll was originally used for stuffing, but bread crumbs are easier.

2 2-pound chickens
1 tablespoon butter or margarine
2 chicken livers
6 slices bread, made into crumbs
1 egg
2 teaspoons chopped fresh parsley
1 teaspoon chopped fresh dill
Salt and freshly ground black pepper
⅔ cup chicken stock

1. Remove the fat from just inside the cavities of the chicken, and discard it. Melt the butter in a small skillet. Pick over the chicken livers and cut away any discolored portions. Add chicken livers, to the butter, and cook until just brown. Chop and set aside.

2. Combine the bread crumbs, egg, herbs, salt and pepper, and mix well. (Chopped mushrooms or onions may be added to the stuffing, if wished.) Mix in the chopped chicken livers.

3. Stuff the cavities of the chickens, and sew up the

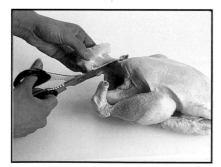

Step 1 Remove the fat from the inside of the cavity of each chicken, and discard it.

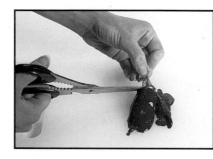

Step 1 Pick over the chicken livers, and remove any discolored parts.

Step 3 Fill the chickens, and sew up the opening with fine thread, using a trussing needle.

openings with fine thread, using a trussing needle. Tie the legs together.

4. Place the chickens in a roasting pan and spread the breasts and legs lightly with more butter. Pour the stock around the chickens, and roast in a preheated 375°F oven for about 55-60 minutes. Baste frequently with the juices during roasting.

5. When the chickens are cooked, remove them from the roasting pan, and keep them warm. Remove the string. Skim any fat from the surface of the pan juices. If a lot of liquid has accumulated, pour into a small saucepan, and reduce over high heat. Pour the juices over the chickens to serve.

Cook's Notes

Time
Preparation takes about 20 minutes, cooking takes, about 55-60 minutes.

Cook's Tip
To check if chicken is cooked, pierce thickest part of thigh with a skewer. Juices should run clear.

Serving Idea
Serve with a cucumber salad or a Polish-style lettuce salad and new potatoes tossed with butter and dill.

CHAPTER 4

NICE & SPICY

SERVES 6

SPICY SPANISH CHICKEN

Chilis, cilantro and sunny tomatoes add
warm Spanish flavor to broiled chicken.

6 boned chicken breasts
Grated rind and juice of 1 lime
2 tablespoons olive oil
Coarsely ground black pepper
6 tablespoons whole grain mustard
2 teaspoons paprika
4 ripe tomatoes, peeled, seeded and quartered
2 shallots, chopped
1 clove garlic, crushed
½ jalapeño pepper or other chili, seeded and chopped
1 teaspoon wine vinegar
Pinch salt
2 tablespoons chopped fresh cilantro
Whole fresh cilantro leaves to garnish

Step 1 Marinate chicken in a shallow dish, turning occasionally to coat.

1. Place chicken breasts in a shallow dish with the lime rind and juice, oil, pepper, mustard and paprika. Marinate for about 1 hour, turning occasionally.

2. To peel tomatoes, drop them into boiling water for about 20 seconds or less depending on ripeness. Place immediately in cold water. Peel should come off easily.

Step 2 Tomatoes peel easily when placed first in boiling water and then in cold.

3. Place the tomatoes, shallots, garlic, chili, vinegar and salt in a food processor, and process until coarsely, chopped. Stir in the cilantro by hand.

4. Place chicken on a rack in a broiler pan, and reserve the marinade. Cook chicken skin-side uppermost for about 7-10 minutes, depending on how close it is to the heat source. Baste frequently with the remaining marinade. Cook other side in the same way. Then sprinkle with salt.

5. Place chicken on serving plates and garnish top with cilantro leaves or sprigs. Serve with a spoonful of the tomato relish on one side.

Step 4 Broil skin side of chicken until brown and crisp before turning pieces over.

Cook's Notes

 **Time**
Preparation takes about 1 hour including marinating, cooking takes 14-20 minutes.

 **Preparation**
Tomato relish can be prepared ahead and kept in the refrigerator.

 Watchpoint
When preparing chilis, wear rubber gloves or at least be sure to wash hands thoroughly after handling them. Do not touch eyes or face before washing hands.

SERVES 4-6

CHICKEN, SAUSAGE AND OKRA STEW

There is an exotic taste to this economical chicken stew.
The garlic sausage adds flavor instantly.

½ cup oil
1 3-pound chicken, cut into 6-8 pieces
1 cup all-purpose flour
1 large onion, finely chopped
1 large green bell pepper, roughly chopped
3 stalks celery, finely chopped
2 cloves garlic, crushed
1½ cups diced garlic sausage
5 cups chicken stock
1 bay leaf
Dash Tabasco
Salt and freshly ground black pepper
4 ounces fresh okra

1. Heat the oil in a large skillet, and brown the chicken on both sides, 3-4 pieces at a time. Transfer the chicken to a plate, and set it aside.

2. Lower the heat under the skillet, and add the flour. Cook over a very low heat for about 30 minutes, stirring constantly until the flour turns a rich, dark brown. Take the skillet off the heat occasionally, so that the flour does not burn.

3. Add the onion, green bell pepper, celery, garlic and sausage to the skillet and cook for about 5 minutes over a very low heat, stirring continuously.

4. Pour on the stock, and stir well. Add the bay leaf, a dash of Tabasco, salt and pepper. Return the chicken to the skillet, cover and cook for about 30 minutes or until the chicken is tender.

5. Top and tail the okra, and cut each into 2-3 pieces. If okra are small, leave whole. Add to chicken, and cook for 10-15 minutes longer. Remove the bay leaf, and serve.

Step 2 Continue cooking over low heat, stirring constantly as the flour begins to brown.

Step 3 When the flour is rich dark brown, add the remaining sauce ingredients.

Cook's Notes

 Time
Preparation takes about 30 minutes, cooking takes about 1 hour 25 minutes.

 Cook's Tip
The oil and flour roux may be made ahead, and kept in the refrigerator to use whenever needed. If the roux is cold, heat the liquid before adding.

 Serving Idea
Serve on a bed of rice.

SERVES 4

EGGPLANT AND CHICKEN CHILLI

This unusual dish is both delicious and filling.

2 medium-sized eggplants
4 tablespoons sesame oil
2 cloves garlic, crushed
4 scallions
1 green chili, finely chopped
12 ounces boned and skinned chicken breast
4 tablespoons light soy sauce
2 tablespoons stock, or water
1 tablespoon tomato paste
1 teaspoon cornstarch
Sugar to taste

1. Cut the eggplant into quarters lengthwise, using a sharp knife. Slice the eggplant quarters into pieces approximately ½ inch thick.

2. Put the eggplant slices into a bowl, and sprinkle liberally with salt. Stir well to coat evenly. Cover with plastic wrap and let sit for 30 minutes.

3. Rinse the eggplant slices very thoroughly under running water, then pat dry with a clean dish cloth.

4. Heat half of the oil in a wok, or large skillet, and over a low heat cook the garlic, until it is soft, but not colored.

5. Add the eggplant slices to the wok, and cook, stirring frequently, for 3-4 minutes.

6. Using a sharp knife, slice the scallions into thin

Step 6 Cut the scallions diagonally into small pieces, approximately ½ inch long.

diagonal strips. Stir the scallions together with the chili into the cooked eggplant, and cook for a further 1 minute. Remove the eggplant and onion from the wok, and set aside, keeping warm.

7. Cut the chicken breast into thin slices with a sharp knife.

8. Heat the remaining oil in the wok, and fry the chicken pieces for approximately 2 minutes, or until they have turned white and are thoroughly cooked.

9. Return the eggplant and onions to the wok and cook, stirring continuously, for 2 minutes, or until heated through completely.

10. Mix together the remaining ingredients, and pour these over the chicken and eggplant in the wok, stirring constantly until the sauce has thickened and cleared. Serve immediately.

Cook's Notes

Time
Preparation takes about 10 minutes plus 30 minutes sitting time. Cooking takes about 15 minutes.

Cook's Tip
The vegetables can be prepared well ahead, but the eggplants should be removed from the salt after 30 minutes, or they will become too dehydrated.

Serving Idea
Serve this dish as part of a more extensive Chinese-style meal.

SERVES 4

SPICY CHICKEN

This is a really aromatic dish, perfect
for special midweek dinner parties.

4 large dry red chilis
½ teaspoon cumin seed
¼ teaspoon fennel seed
2 tablespoons coriander seed
1-inch piece fresh gingerroot, peeled and roughly chopped
1 clove garlic, roughly chopped
Juice of 1 lime
8 chicken thighs or drumsticks, skinned and boned
Salt
2 tablespoons oil

4. Cut the chicken into 1-inch cubes. Stir in the chili paste and a pinch of salt.

5. Let marinate in the refrigerator for 2 hours.

6. Heat the oil in a large skillet and sauté the chicken pieces over a medium heat for 15-20 minutes until firm to the touch and cooked through. Do not be tempted to overcrowd the skillet – they should only be cooked in a single layer. If necessary, cook in batches and keep warm. Serve immediately.

Step 3 Grind the chilis, the dry roasted spices, ginger and garlic to a paste.

Step 1 Soak the dried chilis in boiling water for 5 minutes.

1. Soak the chilis in boiling water for 5 minutes.

2. Meanwhile, put the cumin seed, fennel seed and coriander seed into a dry skillet, and roast over a high heat shaking the pan, until the seeds become slightly colored and give off a spicy aroma.

3. Drain the chilis and put them, with the dry roasted spices, ginger and garlic, into a food processor, coffee grinder, or pestle and mortar, and grind to a paste. Then gradually add the lime juice.

Step 6 Sauté the chicken pieces over a medium heat for 15-20 minutes, or until cooked through. Do not overcrowd the skillet.

Cook's Notes

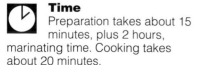

Time
Preparation takes about 15 minutes, plus 2 hours, marinating time. Cooking takes about 20 minutes.

Serving Idea
Serve with a salad of chopped tomatoes, cucumbers and carrot on a bed of lettuce, with thick yogurt on the side.

Cook's Tip
Toasting the whole spices helps to develop their flavor.

SERVES 4-6

CHICKEN MOGHLAI WITH CILANTRO CHUTNEY

The creamy spiciness of the chicken is a good contrast to the hotness of the chutney.

4 tablespoons oil
3 pounds chicken pieces, skinned
1 teaspoon ground cardamom
½ teaspoon ground cinnamon
1 bay leaf
4 cloves
2 onions, finely chopped
1-inch piece fresh gingerroot, grated
4 cloves garlic, crushed
¼ cup ground almonds
2 teaspoons cumin seeds
Pinch cayenne pepper
1¼ cups light cream
6 tablespoons natural yogurt
2 tablespoons roasted cashew nuts
2 tablespoons golden raisins
Salt

Chutney
1½ cups fresh cilantro leaves
1 green chili, seeded and chopped
1 tablespoon lemon juice
Salt and freshly ground black pepper
Pinch sugar
1 tablespoon oil
½ tsp ground coriander

1. To prepare the chicken, heat the oil in a large skillet. Fry the chicken pieces on each side until golden-brown.

2. Remove the chicken, and set aside. Put the cardamom, cinnamon, bay leaf and cloves into the hot oil and meat

Step 7 Stir the yogurt, cashews and golden raisins into the chicken. Heat through gently to plump up the golden raisins, but do not let the mixture boil.

juices, and fry for 30 seconds. Stir in the onions, and fry until soft but not brown.

3. Stir the ginger, garlic, almonds, cumin and cayenne pepper into the onions. Cook gently for 2-3 minutes, then stir in the cream.

4. Return the chicken pieces to the skillet, along with any juices. Cover and simmer over a low heat for 30-40 minutes, or until the chicken is cooked and tender.

5. While the chicken is cooking, prepare the chutney. Put the cilantro leaves, chili, lemon, seasoning and sugar into a blender or food processor, and work to a paste.

6. Heat the oil, and cook the ground coriander for 1 minute. Add this mixture to the processed cilantro leaves, and blend in thoroughly.

7. Just before serving, stir the yogurt, cashews and golden raisins into the chicken. Heat through just enough to plump up the golden raisins, but do not let the mixture boil.

8. Serve at once with the cilantro chutney.

Cook's Notes

 Time
Preparation takes about 25 minutes, cooking takes 30-40 minutes.

 **Preparation**
The cilantro chutney can be prepared using a pestle and mortar, if a blender or food processor is not available.

 Serving Idea
Serve with boiled rice and a cucumber and tomato salad.

SERVES 4-6

CHICKEN TOMATO

Made with a very fragrant selection of spices,
this dish is sure to become a firm favorite.

1 onion, chopped
3 tablespoons oil
1-inch piece cinnamon stick
1 bay leaf
6 cloves
Seeds of 6 small cardamoms
1-inch piece fresh gingerroot, grated
4 cloves garlic, crushed
1 3-pound chicken, cut into 8-10 pieces
1 teaspoon chili powder
1 teaspoon ground cumin
1 teaspoon ground coriander
1 14-ounce can tomatoes, chopped
1 teaspoon salt
2 sprigs fresh cilantro leaves, chopped
2 green chilis, halved and seeded

1. In a large saucepan, fry the onion in the oil, until it
has softened. Add the cinnamon, bay leaf, cloves,
cardamom seeds, ginger and garlic. Cook for 1 minute.

2. Add the chicken pieces to the saucepan. Sprinkle
the chili powder, ground cumin and coriander over the
chicken in the pan. Fry for 2 minutes longer, stirring
continuously, to insure the spices do not burn.

Step 2 Fry the
chicken and spices
together, stirring
continuously, to
prevent the spices
burning.

Step 3 Mix the
canned tomatoes
and remaining
seasonings into the
chicken, stirring
thoroughly to blend
the spices evenly.

3. Stir in the remaining ingredients, mixing well to blend
the spices evenly. Cover the pan, and simmer for 40-
45 minutes, or until the chicken is tender.

Cook's Notes

Time
Preparation takes about 30
minutes, cooking takes
about 40-50 minutes.

Serving Idea
Serve with boiled rice.

SERVES 4-6

CHICKEN TIKKA

Red food coloring gives this dish its
traditional appearance, but the taste will not
be affected if you prefer not to use it.

⅔ cup natural yogurt
1 teaspoon chili powder
2 teaspoons ginger paste
2 teaspoons garlic paste
2 teaspoons garam masala
½ teaspoon salt
¼ teaspoon red food coloring
Juice of 1 lemon
1 3-pound chicken, cut into 8-10 pieces
Oil for brushing

Step 2 Add the
chicken pieces to
the yogurt mixture,
stirring well, to
make sure thay are
evenly coated.

Step 1 In a large
bowl, mix together
the yogurt, chili
powder, ginger and
garlic pastes,
garam masala, salt,
coloring and lemon
juice.

Step 3 Line a
broiler pan with foil
and arrange the
chicken pieces on
this.

1. In a large bowl, mix together the yogurt, chili powder,
ginger and garlic pastes, garam masala, salt, coloring
and lemon juice.

2. Add the chicken pieces to the yogurt mixture, and
mix well to insure they are evenly coated. Cover and chill
for at least 2 hours.

3. Line a broiler pan with foil, and arrange the chicken
pieces on this, together with the yogurt
sauce. Preheat the broiler to moderate, and cook the
chicken pieces for about 8-10 minutes on each side,
brushing with a little oil if necessary, to prevent them
burning.

Cook's Notes

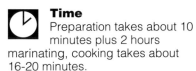 **Time**
Preparation takes about 10
minutes plus 2 hours
marinating, cooking takes about
16-20 minutes.

 **Variation**
Use chicken drumsticks
instead of a whole cut
chicken.

 Preparation
Chicken can be marinated
overnight if wished.

SERVES 6

FLAUTAS

Traditionally, these are long, thin rolls of tortillas with savory fillings, topped with sour cream.

1½ cups skinned, boned and ground or finely chopped chicken
1 tablespoon oil
1 small onion, finely chopped
½ green bell pepper, finely chopped
½-1 chili, seeded and finely chopped
⅓ cup frozen corn
6 black olives, pitted and chopped
½ cup heavy cream
Salt
12 prepared tortillas
Taco sauce, guacamole and sour cream for toppings

1. Use a food processor or meat grinder to prepare the chicken, or chop by hand.

2. Heat the oil in a medium skillet, and add the chicken, onion and green bell pepper. Cook over moderate heat, stirring frequently to break up the pieces of chicken.

3. When the chicken is cooked and the vegetables are softened, add the chili, corn, olives, cream and salt. Bring to a boil over heat and boil rapidly, stirring continuously, to reduce and thicken the cream.

4. Place 2 tortillas on a clean counter, overlapping them by about 2 inches. Spoon some of the chicken mixture onto the tortillas, roll up and secure with toothpicks.

5. Fry the flautas in about ½ inch of oil in a large skillet. Do not allow the tortillas to get very brown. Drain on paper towel.

6. Arrange the flautas on serving plates, and top with sour cream, guacamole and taco sauce.

Step 4 Place tortillas slightly overlapping on counter and fill with chicken.

Step 4 Use toothpicks to secure tortillas.

Step 5 Fry slowly and turn carefully, so that the filling does not leak.

Cook's Notes

Time
Preparation takes about 15 minutes, cooking takes about 15 minutes.

Variation
Green olives, may be substituted for black, and red bell peppers for green.

Serving Idea
Flautas are often served with rice, refried beans and a salad.

SERVES 4

SPICY BARBECUE CHICKEN

Whether you cook this recipe in the oven on a cold winter's evening or
on the barbecue in the height of summer, it is bound to be a success.

4 chicken pieces
⅔ cup maple syrup or clear honey
¼ teaspoon cayenne pepper
½ teaspoon salt
Freshly ground black pepper
2 cloves garlic, crushed
2 tablespoons tomato paste
1 tablespoon Dijon mustard
2 tablespoons lemon juice

Step 3 Spoon enough of the sauce over the chicken to coat each piece well.

Step 1 Lay the chicken pieces in a roasting pan, skinned-side uppermost.

1. Skin the chicken pieces and lay them in a roasting pan, skinned-side uppermost.

2. Meanwhile, mix together the remaining ingredients to make the barbecue sauce.

3. Spoon enough sauce over the chicken to coat each piece well.

4. Bake in a preheated 450°F oven for 30-40 minutes, basting the chicken once or twice with the sauce.

5. Test the chicken, in the thickest part, with a sharp knife. If the juices run clear, it is cooked; if the juices are pink, then return the chicken to the oven for another 5-10 minutes and test again. Serve the extra sauce separately.

Cook's Notes

Time
Preparation takes about 10 minutes, cooking takes about 30-40 minutes.

Variation
You can use this sauce when cooking chicken pieces on the barbecue. It is a good idea to marinate the chicken in the sauce for at least 4 hours before you start the barbecue, to get a really good flavor.

Serving Idea
Serve with jacket potatoes and either a green salad or a selection of seasonal vegetables.

SERVES 4

CHICKEN IN RED PEPPER SAUCE

This recipe blends the exotic spices of the
Far East with the delicate flavour of chicken.

4 large boneless chicken breasts, skinned
2 tablespoons butter
1 tablespoon oil
1 medium onion, roughly chopped
1-inch piece, fresh gingerroot, peeled
3 cloves garlic
¼ cup blanched almonds
Red bell pepper, roughly chopped
1 tablespoon cumin powder
2 teaspoons coriander powder
1 teaspoon turmeric powder
Pinch cayenne pepper
½ teaspoon salt
6 tablespoons vegetable oil
⅔ cup water
3 star anise
2 tablespoons lemon juice
Freshly ground black pepper

1. Cut the chicken breasts into largish pieces about 2 inches long and 1inch wide.

2. Heat the butter and oil in a skillet, add the chicken pieces, and cook for 5 minutes. Remove to a plate.

3. Combine the onion, ginger, garlic, almonds, red bell pepper, cumin, coriander, turmeric, cayenne and salt in a food processor or liquidizer.

4. Blend to a smooth paste. Heat the oil in a large saucepan or deep skillet. Add the paste, and fry for 10-12 minutes.

5. Add the chicken pieces, the water, star anise, lemon juice and black pepper. Cover, reduce the heat, and simmer slowly for 20-25 minutes, or until the chicken is tender. Stir a few times during cooking.

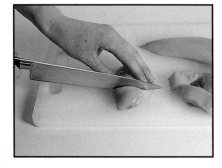

Step 1 Cut the chicken breasts into largish pieces.

Step 4 Blend onion, ginger, garlic, almonds, red bell peppers, cumin, coriander, turmeric, cayenne and salt to a smooth paste.

Step 5 Add chicken pieces, water, star anise, lemon juice and black pepper to the skillet.

Cook's Notes

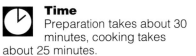

Time
Preparation takes about 30 minutes, cooking takes about 25 minutes.

Serving Idea
Serve with plain boiled or pilau rice.

Buying Guide
Star anise is available from Oriental stores and some large supermarkets. If not available, substitute ¼ teaspoon of Chinese five-spice or fennel seeds.

SERVES 4

AROMATIC CHICKEN CURRY

This isn't quite what you'd expect from a curry, for it is not hot,
yet such voluptuous flavors are more representative of Indian
cooking than dishes which burn the roof of your mouth off.

2 cups finely chopped onion
1 tablespoon granulated sugar
8 whole, unpeeled garlic cloves
1 fresh lime, quartered
1 cinnamon stick
8 cardamom pods
6 whole cloves
2 envelopes powdered saffron, to taste
8 chicken thighs, skinned
2½ cups boiling water
½ cup creamed coconut
Salt and freshly ground black pepper
2-3 bananas, peeled and cut into large chunks

Step 1 Cook the onion in a little oil or butter until very soft. Add the sugar, and cook until caramelized.

1. Cook the onion in a little oil or butter until very soft, then sprinkle over the sugar, and cook over a moderate heat until it has caramelized and the onions are golden-brown.

2. Add the garlic, lime, cinnamon stick, cardamom, cloves and saffron, and stir well. Place the chicken pieces in the saucepan, and pour over the water.

3. Bring to a boil, cover and simmer slowly until the chicken is tender – about 30 minutes.

4. Remove the chicken, and keep warm. Ideally, you should remove the lime, cinnamon stick and the other whole spices.

5. Break up the creamed coconut, and gradually stir the pieces into the liquid, taking care not to let it boil.

Step 5 Gradually stir in the broken-up creamed coconut, then cook over a low heat and do not let it boil.

6. Taste and adjust the seasoning – add extra coconut if you like a thicker or richer sauce, but be careful not to hide the subtle taste of the spices.

7. Return the chicken pieces to the sauce with the pieces of banana. Warm gently for a few minutes, and then serve.

Cook's Notes

Time
Preparation takes about 20 minutes, cooking takes about 40 minutes.

Variation
If you cannot find saffron but like the yellow color, you can substitute turmeric, although it will not give quite the same flavor.

Serving Idea
Serve with lightly fried cashew nuts, mango chutney or natural yogurt with cucumber and mint.

SERVES 6

SPECIAL OCCASION CURRIED CHICKEN

This recipe makes a delicious alternative to plain roasted chicken, and will appeal to the whole family.

1 3½-pound chicken
3 tablespoons butter
1 onion, finely chopped
2 cloves garlic, crushed
1-inch piece fresh gingerroot, peeled and finely grated
3 tablespoons curry powder
1 small green chili, deseeded and finely chopped
2 cups chicken stock
3 tablespoons mango chutney
1 tablespoon soft brown sugar
Juice of ½ lemon
Good pinch garam masala
Boiled rice, to serve

1. Put the chicken in a deep roasting dish or casserole which has a tight-fitting lid.

2. Melt the butter in a saucepan, and sauté the onion and garlic over a low heat until soft.

3. Add the ginger, curry powder and chopped chili, and

Step 2 Sauté the onion and garlic over a low heat until soft.

Step 3 Add the stock, mango chutney, sugar and lemon juice, and simmer uncovered for 30 minutes.

Step 4 Pour the sauce over the chicken and cook for 2½ hours, basting occasionally with the juices in the dish.

cook for 2 minutes. Add the stock, mango chutney, sugar and lemon juice, and simmer, uncovered, for 30 minutes.

4. Pour this sauce over the chicken, cover and cook in a preheated 325°F oven for 2½ hours, basting the chicken occasionally with the juices in the dish. Then remove the lid, and return to the oven for 30 minutes longer to let the sauce evaporate and thicken.

5. Sprinkle with garam masala, and serve with boiled rice.

Cook's Notes

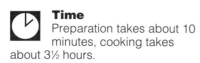

Time
Preparation takes about 10 minutes, cooking takes about 3½ hours.

Variation
You can substitute a few drops of chili sauce for the fresh chili.

Serving Idea
As an alternative to boiled rice, serve with naan bread, and perhaps a spicy sambal, or chutney.

CHAPTER 5

ENTERTAINING

SERVES 2

HOT CHICKEN WITH PEACHES

Tangy with fresh ginger and fruit vinegar, this combination
makes a delicious summer dinner party dish.

12 ounces boneless chicken meat
2 tablespoons fruit vinegar (or cider vinegar)
1 tablespoon finely grated fresh gingerroot
¾-1 pound fresh peaches
2 tablespoons oil
2 tablespoons dry white wine
1 tablespoon sliced fresh mint
Salt and freshly ground black pepper

1. If using breast meat, cut into 3 or 4 long, thin strips. If using thigh or drumstick meat, keep in large pieces.

2. Put the chicken into a shallow dish with the fruit or cider vinegar and the grated ginger. Cover and let marinate in a cool place for a few hours.

3. Meanwhile, drop the peaches into boiling water for 2 minutes, then peel and cut into segments.

4. Drain the marinade from the chicken, and reserve.

5. Heat the oil in a large skillet, then add the chicken and cook over medium heat for 5-7 minutes, turning from time to time, until cooked through.

6. Remove the chicken to a warm dish. Pour the marinade and the wine into the skillet. Season and, when hot, slide in the peaches, and heat through without stirring.

7. Sprinkle the mint leaves into this hot liquid, and the moment they have wilted, remove the skillet from the heat. Serve the chicken topped with the peaches and with the hot vinaigrette strained over the combination.

Step 3 Drop the peaches into boiling water for 2 minutes, then peel and cut into segments.

Step 2 Put the sliced chicken into a shallow dish to marinate with the vinegar and ginger.

Step 5 Sauté the chicken in a large skillet for 5-7 minutes, or until cooked through.

 Cook's Notes

Time
Preparation takes about 30 minutes, plus a minimum of 2 hours, marinating time. Cooking takes about 15 minutes.

Variation
If you like a more savory flavor, soften ¼ cup of very finely chopped onion and/or a little garlic in the oil before adding the chicken, but do not let either burn.

Serving Idea
Serve this dish on top of a mixed salad, or accompanied by a selection of plainly cooked, seasonal vegetables.

SERVES 4

POULET SAUTÉ VALLÉE D'AUGE

This dish contains all the ingredients that Normandy
is famous for – butter, cream, apples and Calvados.

¼ cup butter or margarine
2 tablespoons oil
1 3-pound chicken, cut into eight pieces
4 tablespoons Calvados
6 tablespoons chicken stock
2 eating apples, peeled, cored and coarsely chopped
1 shallot, finely chopped
2 stalks celery, finely chopped
½ teaspoon dried thyme, crumbled
2 egg yolks, lightly beaten
6 tablespoons heavy cream
Salt and freshly ground black pepper

Garnish
2 tablespoons butter
2 eating apples, quartered, cored and cut into cubes
Sugar
1 bunch watercress or fresh small parsley sprigs

Step 1 Brown the chicken a few pieces at a time, skin side down first.

Step 7 Cook diced apple until it begins to caramelise.

1. Melt half the butter and all of the oil in a large skillet over moderate heat. When the foam begins to subside, brown the chicken, a few pieces at a time, skin-side down first. When all the chicken is browned, pour off most of the fat from the skillet and return the chicken to the skillet.

2. Pour the Calvados into the skillet and warm over a low heat. Ignite with a match, shake the pan gently until the flames subside.

3. Pour over the stock, and scrape up any browned chicken juices from the bottom of the skillet. Set the chicken aside.

4. Melt the remaining butter in a small saucepan or skillet. Cook the chopped apples, shallot and celery and the thyme for about 10 minutes, or until soft but not brown.

5. Spoon over the chicken, and return the pan to the

high heat. Bring to a boil, then reduce heat, cover the pan, and simmer for 50 minutes.

6. When the chicken is cooked, beat the eggs and cream together. With a whisk, gradually beat in some of the hot sauce. Pour the mixture back into a saucepan, and cook over a low heat for 2-3 minutes, stirring constantly until the sauce thickens and coats the back of a spoon. Season to taste, and set aside while preparing the garnish.

7. Put the butter in a small skillet and when foaming, add the apple. Toss over a high heat until beginning to soften. Sprinkle with sugar, and cook until the apple begins to caramelise.

8. To serve, coat the chicken with the sauce, and garnish with watercress or parsley. Spoon the caramelized apples over the chicken.

Cook's Notes

Time
Preparation takes 25-20 minutes, cooking takes 55-60 minutes.

Watchpoint
Do not allow the sauce to boil after the egg and cream is added, or it will curdle.

Serving Idea
Serve with sauté potatoes and fresh young peas.

SERVES 4-6

VENETIAN CHICKEN

This elegant dinner party dish incorporates traditional Italian ingredients.
It is a delicious recipe which can't fail to impress your guests.

1 tablespoon olive oil
2 tablespoons butter
1 onion, finely sliced
2 cloves garlic, crushed
1 pound boneless chicken breasts, skinned and cut
   into ½-inch cubes
1 teaspoon dried oregano
Generous 1 cup Italian risotto rice
1 tablespoon tomato paste
5 cups good chicken stock
Splash white wine
Salt and freshly ground black pepper
6 tomatoes, peeled, deseeded and chopped
10 pitted black olives, halved
2 tablespoons chopped fresh parsley
½ cup of grated parmesan cheese

1. Heat the oil and butter in a large skillet and sauté the onion and garlic over a low heat until soft and lightly browned.

2. Add the diced chicken, and cook until pale brown. Add the oregano and rice, and cook for 1 minute until the rice is transparent, then add the tomato paste, stock and wine.

3. Season with salt and pepper, and stir well. Do not be tempted to stir again during cooking, because this would make the rice sticky.

4. Cook over a very low heat for about 25-30 minutes, until all the stock has been absorbed, but the rice still has a slight bite to it.

5. Lightly fork in the tomatoes, olives and chopped parsley, cook for 2 minutes, and serve sprinkled with Parmesan cheese.

Step 1 Sauté the onion and garlic over a low heat until soft and lightly browned.

Step 2 Add the diced chicken, and sauté until lightly browned.

Step 5 Lightly fork in the tomatoes, olives and chopped parsley. Cook for 2 minutes.

Cook's Notes

Time
Preparation takes about 15 minutes, cooking takes about 30 minutes.

Variation
If you prefer, you can substitute a can of tomatoes, drained and chopped, for the fresh tomatoes.

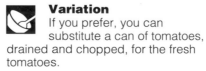
Serving Idea
Serve with a chilled white wine – Frascati complements this dish very well. Accompany with a mixed green salad.

SERVES 4

CHICKEN WITH BLACKCURRANT SAUCE

The sharp tang of blackcurrants makes an ideal partner for lightly cooked chicken.

4 chicken breasts, skinned and boned
3 tablespoons sesame oil
1¼ cups fresh blackcurrants
Juice of 1 orange
⅔ cup red wine
Sugar to taste
Orange slices and fresh blackcurrants to garnish

1. Season the chicken breasts with a little salt. Heat the oil in a shallow skillet.

Step 2 Slowly fry the chicken breasts in the hot oil until they are golden-brown on all sides.

Step 5 Press the blackcurrant purée through a fine nylon sieve with a wooden spoon, to remove all the pips and skins.

Step 6 Simmer the sieved fruit purée until it has thickened and the liquid has reduced.

2. Slowly fry the chicken breasts for 6-8 minutes on each side, until they are golden-brown and tender.

3. Meanwhile, put the blackcurrants into a small pan, along with the orange juice and red wine. Bring to a boil, then cover and simmer slowly until the blackcurrants are soft.

4. Using a liquidizer or food processor, blend the blackcurrants and the cooking juice for 30 seconds.

5. Rub the blended purée through a fine nylon strainer with

the back of a spoon, pressing the fruit through to reserve all the juice and pulp but leaving the seeds in the strainer.

6. Put the strained purée into a small saucepan and heat slowly, stirring constantly until the liquid has reduced and the sauce is thick and smooth, adding a little sugar to sweeten if necessary.

7. Arrange the chicken breasts on a serving dish, and spoon the blackcurrant sauce over. Garnish with orange slices and fresh blackcurrants.

Cook's Notes

Time
Preparation takes 15 minutes, cooking takes about 20 minutes.

Preparation
To test if the chicken breasts are cooked, insert a skewer into the thickest part, then press gently; if the juices run clear, the chicken is cooked.

Variation
Use blackberries instead of blackcurrants in this recipe.

SERVES 4

ROAST CHICKEN WITH GARLIC AND HERB SAUCE

This dinner party dish is extremely impressive and yet very easy.

1 medium lemon
1½ cups garlic – and herb-flavoured cream cheese
1 3-pound roasting chicken
2 small bay leaves

1. Grate the lemon zest directly into a small bowl and mash up 1 cup of the cheese evenly with this.

2. Ease this mixture evenly and gently between the breast and the skin of the bird.

Step 2 Ease the cream cheese under the skin of the chicken to cover the breast meat in an even layer.

3. Put the bay leaves into the chicken cavity, and put the chicken into a roasting bag, or enclose in foil.

4. Squeeze the lemon, and pour the juice into the bag; put the lemon halves into the cavity of the chicken.

5. Seal and slash the roasting bag as directed, and bake in a preheated 375°F oven for 20 minutes per pound, plus 20 minutes extra.

6. Cut the bag open, and pour all the juices, including those inside the chicken, into a measuring jug.

Step 6 Pour all the juices into a measuring jug.

7. Now carefully pour away the fat which will have risen to the top until you have about ⅔ cup of well-flavored stock, reheat slowly and then remove from heat.

8. Chop the remaining cheese into pieces, and whisk into the warm sauce. Carve the chicken, and pour the sauce over immediately.

Step 8 Cut up the remaining cheese and whisk the pieces into the warm sauce.

Cook's Notes

Time
Preparation takes about 20 minutes, cooking takes about 1 hour 20 minutes.

Serving Idea
A chilled rosé wine from California is an excellent accompaniment to this dish.

Variation
You could try ringing the changes by using bell pepper-flavored cheese or by combining two flavors, using one for the stuffing and one for the sauce.

SERVES 4

POUSSINS WITH DEVILED SAUCE

Although this recipe takes quite a time to prepare,
the end result will make your effort worthwhile.

4 single (small) poussins
1 teaspoon each of paprika, mustard powder and
    ground ginger
½ teaspoon ground turmeric
¼ teaspoon ground allspice
¼ cup butter
2 tablespoons chili sauce
1 tablespoon plum chutney
1 tablespoon brown sauce
1 tablespoon Worcestershire sauce
1 tablespoon soy sauce
Dash Tabasco sauce
3 tablespoons chicken stock

1. Tie the legs of each poussin together.

2. Put the paprika, mustard and ginger, turmeric and allspice, into a small bowl, and mix together well.

3. Rub the spice mixture evenly all over the poussins, pushing some behind the wings and into the joints, then chill them for at least 1 hour.

4. Arrange the poussins in a roasting pan. Melt the butter, and brush it evenly over the birds. Roast in a preheated 350°F oven for 20 minutes, brushing with the roasting juices during this time.

5. Put the chili sauce, plum chutney, brown sauce, Worcestershire sauce, soy sauce, Tabasco and chicken stock into a small bowl, and mix well.

6. Brush about half of this sauce over the poussins. Return to the oven, and cook for 20-30 minutes longer.

7. Brush the poussins twice more with the remaining sauce mixture during this final cooking time, so that the skins become brown and crisp.

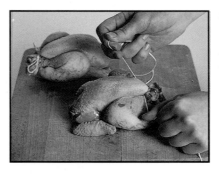

Step 1 Tie the legs of each poussin together with trussing thread.

Step 3 Rub the poussins all over with the spice mixture, pressing it down into the wings and joints.

Cook's Notes

Time
Preparation takes about 20 minutes, plus 1 hour chilling time. Cooking takes 40-50 minutes, depending on the size of the poussins.

Serving Idea
Serve with fresh cooked pasta and a large salad.

Cook's Tip
The poussins could be chilled overnight with the spices.

SERVES 4

LIME-ROASTED CHICKEN

Chicken breast, cooked with the tangy flavor
of limes, makes the perfect summer meal.

4 chicken breasts, each weighing about 8 ounces
Salt and freshly ground black pepper
4 limes
2 teaspoons white wine vinegar
5 tablespoons olive oil
2 teaspoons chopped fresh basil

1. Rub the chicken breasts all over with salt and pepper. Place in a shallow ovenproof dish, and set aside.

2. Remove the zest from 2 of the limes, using a zester. Cut these 2 limes in half, and squeeze the juice.

3. Add lime juice to the vinegar and 4 tablespoons of the olive oil in a small dish, along with the zest, and mix well.

4. Pour the oil and lime juice mixture over the chicken breasts

in the dish. Cover and chill for about 4 hours, or overnight.

5. Remove the covering from the dish in which the chicken is marinating, and baste the chicken well with the marinade mixture. Place into a preheated 375°F oven and cook for 30-35 minutes, or until the chicken is well roasted and tender.

6. Meantime, cut off all the rind and white pith from the remaining 2 limes with a sharp knife, and cut the limes into thin slices.

7. Heat the remaining oil in a small skillet and add the lime slices and basil. Cook quickly for 1 minute, or until the fragrance rises up from the basil and the limes just begin to soften.

8. Serve the chicken breasts on a serving platter, garnished with the fried lime slices and a little extra fresh basil, if wished.

Step 5 After marinating for 4 hours, the chicken breasts will look slightly cooked, and the meat will have turned a pale opaque color.

Step 7 Fry the lime slices very quickly in the hot oil until they just begin to soften.

Cook's Notes

 Time
Preparation takes 25 minutes, plus at least 4 hours' marinating time. Cooking takes 40 minutes.

 Preparation
The chicken can be prepared ahead and marinated overnight.

Variation
Use lemons instead of limes, and thyme instead of basil.

Watchpoint
Let the chicken sit about 30 minutes to come to room temperature before cooking.

SERVES 4

CHICKEN WITH WALNUTS & CELERY

Oyster sauce lends a subtle, slightly salty taste to this Cantonese dish.

8 ounces boned chicken, cut into 1-inch pieces
2 teaspoons soy sauce
2 teaspoons brandy
1 teaspoon cornstarch
Salt and freshly ground black pepper
2 tbsps oil
1 clove garlic
1 cup walnut halves
3 stalks celery
2 teaspoons oyster sauce
⅔ cup water or chicken stock

Step 3 Add the walnuts to the wok, and cook until they are crisp.

Step 4 Use a large, sharp knife to cut the celery on the diagonal into thin slices.

Step 3 Stir-fry the chicken until cooked but not brown.

batches. Stir-fry quickly without letting the chicken brown. Remove the chicken, and add the walnuts to the wok. Cook for about 2 minutes until the walnuts are slightly brown and crisp.

1. Combine the chicken with the soy sauce, brandy, cornstarch, salt and pepper.

2. Heat a wok, and add the oil and garlic. Cook for about 1 minute to flavor the oil.

3. Remove the garlic, and add the chicken in two

4. Slice the celery diagonally, add to the wok, and cook for about 1 minute. Add the oyster sauce and water, and bring to a boil. When boiling, return the chicken to the wok, and stir to coat all the ingredients well. Serve immediately.

Cook's Notes

 **Time**
Preparation takes about 20 minutes, cooking takes about 8 minutes.

Watchpoint
Nuts can burn very easily. Stir them constantly for even browning.

Variation
Almonds or cashew nuts may be used instead of the walnuts. Add along with the celery.

SERVES 4

MARINATED CHICKEN WITH WALNUT SAUCE

Offer your guests a walnut sauce that tastes delicious and is very easy to make.

2 2-pound chickens, cut in half

Marinade
⅔ cup olive oil
Grated rind and juice of 2 lemons
1 tablespoon chopped fresh oregano
Pinch ground cumin
1 tbsp chopped fresh parsley
2 teaspoons chopped fresh thyme
Salt and freshly ground black pepper
Pinch sugar

Walnut Sauce
2 cloves garlic, roughly chopped
4 slices bread, crusts removed, soaked in water for
   10 minutes
2 tablespoons white wine vinegar
4-5 tablespoons olive oil
1-2 tablespoons water (optional)
Salt and freshly ground black pepper
¾ cup ground walnuts

Step 1 Remove the backbone from the chickens using a pair of sharp poultry shears or a cleaver.

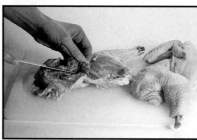

Step 1 Cut away some of the ribcage to make the chickens easier to flatten with a meat mallet or rolling pin.

1. Remove the backbones from the chickens with poultry shears. Bend the legs backward to break the ball and socket joint. Cut away some of the rib cage with a sharp knife. Flatten the chickens slightly with a meat mallet or rolling pin. Mix together the marinating ingredients in a large, shallow dish or a large plastic bag. Add the chickens, and turn to coat. If using a plastic bag, fasten securely and place in a dish to catch any drips. Chill for at least 4 hours or overnight.

2. Place the chickens on the rack of a broiler pan, and cook under low heat for about 30 minutes, turning and basting frequently with the marinade. Raise the heat, and cook for 10 minutes longer, skin-side up, to brown well.

3. Meanwhile, place the garlic in a food processor, and squeeze the bread to remove the water. Add the bread to the food processor, along with the vinegar. With the machine running, pour the oil through the funnel in a thin, steady stream. Add water if necessary to bring the sauce to coating consistency. Add salt and pepper, and stir in the walnuts by hand. When the chicken is cooked, remove to a serving dish, and pour over any remaining marinade. Serve with the walnut sauce.

Cook's Notes

Time
Preparation takes 30 minutes, plus at least 4 hours, marinating time, cooking takes about 40 minutes.

Cook's Tip
If the broiler does not have an adjustable setting, precook the chicken in the oven for about 30 minutes, and broil for the remaining time until cooked.

Serving Idea
Garnish with lemon wedges and sprigs of parsley or other fresh herbs, if wished. Serve with rice and a green or tomato salad.

SERVES 4

CHICKEN WITH RED BELL PEPPERS

Easy as this recipe is, it looks and
tastes good enough for any guests.

4 large red bell peppers
4 skinned and boned chicken breasts
1½ tablespoons oil
Salt and freshly ground black pepper
1 clove garlic, finely chopped
3 tablespoons white wine vinegar
2 scallions, finely chopped
Sage leaves for garnish

5. Heat the oil in a large skillet. Season the chicken breasts on both sides, and place in the hot oil. Cook for 5 minutes, turn over and cook until tender and lightly browned. Remove the chicken, and keep it warm.

6. Add the bell pepper strips, garlic, vinegar and scallions to the skillet, and cook briefly until the vinegar loses its strong aroma.

7. Place the chicken breasts on serving plates. Spoon over the pan juices.

8. Arrange the bell pepper mixture with the chicken, and garnish with the sage leaves.

Step 1 Flatten the bell peppers with the palm of your hand, and brush them with oil.

1. Cut the bell peppers in half lengthwise, and remove the stems, cores and seeds. Flatten the bell peppers with the palm of your hand, and brush the skin sides lightly with some oil.

2. Place the bell peppers skin-side up on the rack of a preheated broiler and cook about 2 inches away from the heat source until the skins are well blistered and charred.

3. Wrap the bell peppers in a clean towel, and let them sit until cool. Peel off the skins with a small vegetable knife. Cut the bell peppers into thin strips, and set aside.

4. Place the chicken breasts between two sheets of dampened baking parchment and flatten by hitting with a rolling pin or meat mallet.

Step 2 Cook the bell peppers until the skins are blistered and well charred.

Step 3 Peel off the skins using a small vegetable knife.

Cook's Notes

 Time
Preparation takes about 35-40 minutes, cooking takes about 10 minutes to char the bell peppers and about 20 minutes to finish the dish.

 Variation
For convenience, the dish may be prepared with canned pimento caps instead of red peppers. These will be softer so cook the garlic, vinegar and onions to soften, and then add pimento.

$ **Buying Guide**
If fresh sage is unavailable, substitute cilantro or parsley leaves as a garnish.

SERVES 4

COQ AU VIN

Originating from the Burgundy region this dish is
probably the most famous chicken recipe in all of France.
It is very rich, definitely a cold weather meal.

10 slices thick-cut streaky bacon
2 cups water
12-16 pearl onions or shallots
2 tablespoons butter or margarine
8 ounces mushrooms, left whole if small, quartered
   if large
1 3-pound chicken, cut into eight pieces
2 cups dry red wine
3 tablspoons brandy
1 bouquet garni
1 clove garlic, crushed
3 tablespoons all-purpose flour
2 cups chicken stock
Salt and freshly ground blackpepper
4 slices bread, crusts removed
Oil for frying
2 tablespoons chopped fresh parsley

1. Cut the bacon into strips about ¼ inch thick. Bring
the water to a boil and blanch the bacon by simmering
for 5 minutes. Remove the bacon with a draining spoon
and dry on paper towels. Re-boil the water and add the
onions. Let them boil rapidly for 2-3 minutes and then
plunge into cold water and peel. Set the onions aside
with the bacon.

2. Melt half the butter in a large skillet over moderate
heat, and add the bacon and onions. Sauté over high
heat, stirring frequently and shaking the pan, until the
bacon and onions are golden-brown. Remove them
with a draining spoon, and leave on paper towels. Add
the remaining butter to the saucepan, and cook the
mushrooms for 1-2 minutes. Remove them, and set
aside with the onions and bacon.

3. Reheat the skillet and brown the chicken, a few
pieces at a time. When all the chicken is browned,
transfer it to a large ovenproof casserole.

Step 1 Cut the
bacon into small
strips and blanch
to remove excess
salt.

4. Pour the wine into a small saucepan, and boil to
reduce to about 1¼ cups. Pour the brandy over
the chicken, and warm over a low heat. Ignite with a
match, and shake the casserole carefully until the flames
die down. Add the bouquet garni and garlic to the
casserole.

5. Pour off all but 1 tablespoon of fat from the skillet and
stir in the flour. Cook over a low heat, scraping up any
of the browned chicken juices from the bottom of the
pan. Stir in the reduced wine, and add the stock. Bring
the sauce to a boil over a high heat, stirring constantly
until thickened. Strain over the chicken in the casserole
and cover tightly.

6. Place in a preheated 350°F oven, and cook for 20
minutes. After that time, add the bacon, onions and
mushrooms, and cook for 15-20 minutes longer, or until
the chicken is tender. Remove the bouquet garni, and
season with salt and pepper.

7. Cut each of the bread slices into 4 triangles. Heat
enough oil in a large skillet to cover the triangles of
bread. When the oil is very hot, add the bread triangles,
two at a time, and fry until golden-brown and crisp. Drain
on paper towels. To serve, arrange the chicken in a
deep dish, pour over the sauce and vegetables, and
arrange the fried bread croûtes around the outside of
the dish. Sprinkle with chopped parsley.

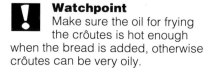

Cook's Notes

 Time
Preparation takes 30-40
minutes, cooking takes about
50 minutes.

! **Watchpoint**
Make sure the oil for frying
the croûtes is hot enough
when the bread is added, otherwise
croûtes can be very oily.

 Cook's Tip
Blanching the bacon in boiling
water removes excess
saltiness. Boiling the onions makes
them easier to peel.

SERVES 4

SPRING CHICKEN WITH BITTER CHOCOLATE SAUCE

Unsweetened chocolate lends a delightfully mysterious flavor to a savory sauce.

4 tablespoons olive oil
4 single (small) poussins
Salt and freshly ground black pepper
3 tablespoons all-purpose flour
1 clove garlic, crushed
1¼ cups chicken stock
4 tablespoons dry white wine
2 teaspoons grated unsweetened cooking chocolate,
Lemon slices to garnish

Step 2 Cook the flour in the oil until it turns a pale straw color.

Step 1 Brown the poussins in the hot oil, turning carefully to avoid tearing the skin.

Step 5 Stir the grated chocolate into the sauce and cook over low heat to melt it.

1. Heat the oil in a heavy-bottomed skillet or casserole. Season the poussins, and place them, breast-side down first, in the hot oil. Cook until golden-brown on all sides, turning frequently.

2. Transfer the poussins to a plate, and add flour to the casserole. Cook a pale straw color.

3. Add the garlic, and cook to soften. Pour on the stock gradually, mixing well. Add the wine, and bring to a boil.

4. Reduce to simmering, replace the poussins, and cover the casserole. Cook for 30-40 minutes, or until the poussins are tender.

5. Transfer the cooked poussins to a serving dish, and skim any fat from the surface of the sauce. Add the grated chocolate, and cook, stirring quickly, over a low heat for 2-3 minutes. Pour some of the sauce over the poussins, and garnish with lemon slices. Serve the remaining sauce separately.

Cook's Notes

 Time
Preparation takes about 20 minutes, cooking takes about 35-45 minutes.

 Buying Guide
Unsweetened cooking chocolate is not the same as plain chocolate, which must not be used as a substitute. Unsweetened chocolate is available in large supermarkets and speciality shops.

Serving Idea
Serve with rice and a vegetable such as peas or asparagus, or with a green salad.

SERVES 4

SPATCHCOCKED POUSSINS WITH MUSTARD GLAZE

This is a very eye-catching dish and very simple to prepare.

2 double (large) poussins, each weighing
  about 1½ pounds
½ cup butter, softened
2 tablespoons whole grain mustard
2 teaspoons sugar
Salt and freshly ground black pepper
Bunch watercress to garnish

1. To "spatchcock" the poussins, turn each one over, and cut through flesh and bone from tail to neck along one side of the backbone. Then flip over so that the skin side is uppermost.

2. Open the bird out flat, and press along the breastbone with the heel of your hand to flatten it thoroughly.

3. Lay the birds bony-side uppermost, and broil for 7-10 minutes.

4. Meanwhile, mix the butter with the mustard and sugar. Turn the birds over, and spread with the mustard butter.

5. Season with salt and pepper, and broil for another 10-12 minutes, or until cooked through and deep brown. To serve, cut the poussins in half along the breast bones, and garnish with watercress.

Step 3 Open the poussins out flat, skin-side up, and flatten the breast bone with the heel of your hand.

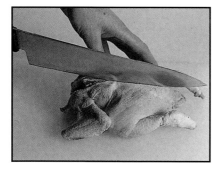

Step 2 Turn each poussin upside down, and cut in half from tail to neck along one side of the backbone.

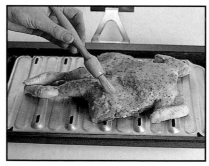

Step 5 Brush the skin side of the poussins with the butter, mustard and sugar glaze.

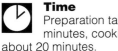 *Cook's Notes*

Time Preparation takes about 20 minutes, cooking takes about 20 minutes.	**Cook's Tip** The poussins can be threaded onto long skewers to help turning over when broiling.

 Serving Idea A chilled, light white wine goes very well with this dish.

SERVES 4

CHICKEN IN MUSTARD AND BRANDY SAUCE

This dish is a real dinner party dazzler.
It tastes delicious and doesn't take long to prepare.

2 tablespoons butter
8 chicken thighs
5 large garlic cloves, unpeeled
5 tablespoons wine vinegar
1¼ cups dry white wine
2 tablespoons brandy
2 teaspoons Dijon mustard
1 heaped teaspoon tomato paste
1¼ cups heavy cream
2 tomatoes, peeled and deseeded

Step 1 Brown the chicken on both sides, and add unpeeled garlic cloves.

1. Melt the butter in a large, heavy bottomed skillet. Fry the chicken thighs on both sides to brown them evenly. Add the unpeeled garlic cloves, and reduce the heat.

2. Cover the skillet and cook gently for 20 minutes, or until the chicken is tender.

3. Pour out all but 1 tablespoon of fat from the skillet and add the vinegar, stirring well and scraping up any browned juices from the bottom.

4. Boil rapidly until the liquid is reduced to about 2 tablespoons.

5. Lift out the chicken and keep warm.

6. Add the wine, brandy, mustard and tomato paste to the skillet. Mix well, and boil rapidly for 5 minutes, or until reduced to a thick sauce.

7. In a heavy saucepan, boil the cream until reduced by half, stirring frequently to prevent it burning. Remove from the heat.

Step 8 Strain the sauce into the cream, pressing the garlic well.

8. Strain the vinegar sauce into the cream, pressing the garlic cloves well to remove the pulp. Season with salt and black pepper.

9. Cut the deseeded tomatoes into thin strips, and stir into the sauce. Reheat the sauce if necessary.

10. Arrange the chicken on a hot serving dish, and spoon over the sauce to serve.

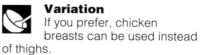
Cook's Notes

Time
Preparation takes about 25 minutes, cooking takes about 30 minutes.

Variation
If you prefer, chicken breasts can be used instead of thighs.

Serving Ideas
Serve with new or sautéed potatoes and zucchini.

SERVES 6

CHICKEN WITH CHERRIES

Canned cherries make an easy
sauce that really dresses up chicken.

4 tablespoons oil
6 chicken breasts, skinned and boned
1 sprig fresh rosemary
Grated rind and juice of ½ lemon
⅔ cup red wine
Salt and freshly ground black pepper
1 1-pound can black cherries, pitted
2 teaspoons cornstarch

Step 1 Cook the chicken breasts until just lightly browned. Watch carefully, as skinned chicken will dry out easily.

1. Heat the oil in a skillet over a moderate heat. Add the chicken breasts, skinned-side down first. Cook until just lightly browned. Turn over, and cook the second side for about 2 minutes.

2. Remove any oil remaining in the skillet and add the rosemary, lemon rind, wine, and salt and pepper. Bring to a boil and then lower the heat.

3. Add the cherries and their juice. Cook, covered, for 15 minutes, or until the chicken is tender. Remove the chicken and cherries, and keep them warm. Discard the rosemary.

4. Mix the cornstarch and lemon juice. Add several spoonfuls of the hot sauce to the cornstarch mixture. Return the mixture to the skillet and bring to a boil, stirring constantly, until thickened and cleared.

5. Pour the sauce over the chicken and cherries. Heat through, and serve.

Cook's Notes

Time
Preparation takes about 10 minutes and cooking takes about 20 minutes.

Preparation
Serve the chicken dish on the day that it is cooked – it does not keep well.

Serving Idea
Serve with rice, and accompany with a green vegetable, such as lightly steamed snow peas.

SERVES 4

TOMATO POUSSINS WITH CILANTRO

A wonderful combination of flavors makes
this an excellent dinner party dish.

4 single (small) poussins
1 envelope powdered saffron
8 ounce can tomatoes, whole or chopped
½ cup fresh cilantro, leaves and stalks
2 large cloves garlic
¼ cup butter
Salt and freshly ground black pepper

Step 2 Brush the poussins all over with the saffron mixture.

Step 1 Trim off any loose skin, and cut the "parson's noses" from the poussins.

Step 3 Put most of the roughly chopped cilantro into the cavities of the poussins.

1. Trim the birds of any loose skin and "parson's noses".

2. Dissolve the saffron in a little of the juice from the tomatoes, and brush the birds all over with this. Take care when handling saffron, as it stains – ideally, wear a pair of rubber gloves.

3. Fold the cilantro a few times, chop roughly, and put most of it into the cavities of the birds.

4. Put the birds into a baking dish just large enough to accommodate them, with the tomatoes.

5. Crush the garlic over them, then dot with butter, and sprinkle with the remaining cilantro.

6. Season lightly with salt and pepper, turn the birds onto their sides, and cover the dish with a dome of foil.

7. Bake in a preheated 350°F oven for 30-40 minutes, or until the birds are completely cooked, turning them onto their other side halfway through the cooking time.

Cook's Notes

Time
Preparation takes about 15 minutes, cooking takes about 40 minutes.

Serving Idea
Serve with new potatoes, carrots and snow peas.

Variation
If wished, substitute the saffron with turmeric, which will still give color, but the flavor will not be the same.

SERVES 4

CHICKEN AND SHRIMP WITH PASTA IN A CREAM SAUCE

The combination of chicken and seafood is always
a success when having guests for dinner.

1 pound boneless chicken breasts
6 tablespoons white wine
Salt and freshly ground black pepper
1¼ cups shelled fava beans (before removing outer skins)
2 tablespoons butter
½ cup shelled cooked shrimp
¼ cup all-purpose flour
1¼ cups light cream
1 heaped tablespoon chopped fresh dill or
  1 teaspoon dried dill weed
Cooked pasta, to serve

Step 1 Cut chicken breasts, across the grain, into ¾-inch wide strips.

1. Cut the chicken breast into strips about ¾ inch wide. Put them into a shallow ovenproof dish, pour over the wine, and season with salt and pepper.

2. Cover and cook in a preheated 350°F oven for about 25 minutes, until tender. Let cool, then cut the strips in half lengthwise.

3. Strain and reserve the cooking liquid.

4. Cook the beans until just tender, then drain and remove the white outer skins. (If you use frozen fava beans, the skins can be slipped off before cooking, as the beans have already been blanched.)

5. Melt the butter over a low heat, and add the shrimps. Stir in the flour, and blend carefully. Cooking for 1-2 minutes, stirring constantly.

6. Make the cream up to 2 cups using the reserved cooking liquid. Off the heat, stir this into the shrimp, and return to a low heat, stirring until you have a smooth sauce.

7. Add the dill and the shelled beans, and season to taste. Stir in the chicken strips, heat slowly until warmed and serve with pasta.

Step 5 Stir the flour into the melted butter and shrimp and blend carefully over a low heat.

Step 7 Stir in the chicken strips, and heat slowly to warm through.

Cook's Notes

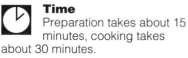

Time
Preparation takes about 15 minutes, cooking takes about 30 minutes.

Variation
This recipe can be made with ready-cooked chicken.

Serving Idea
Serve with a green side salad. A chilled white wine always complements pasta.

SERVES 4

PECAN CHICKEN

Pecans can be used in both sweet and savory dishes.
Here their rich, sweet taste complements a stuffing for chicken.

4 boneless chicken breasts
3 tablespoons butter or margarine
1 small onion, finely chopped
⅓ cup pork sausage meat
1½ cups fresh bread crumbs
1 teaspoon chopped fresh thyme
1 teaspoon chopped fresh parsley
1 small egg, lightly beaten
1 cup pecan halves
1¼ cups chicken stock
1 tablespoon all-purpose flour
2 tablespoons sherry
Salt and freshly ground black pepper
Chopped fresh parsley or 1 bunch watercress to
    garnish

1. Cut a small pocket in the thick side of each chicken breast using a small knife.

2. Melt 1 tablespoon of the butter in a small saucepan, and add the onion. Cook for a few minutes over a low heat to soften. Add the sausage meat, and turn up the heat to brown. Break up the sausage meat with a fork as it cooks.

3. Drain off excess fat, and add the bread crumbs, herbs and a pinch of salt and pepper to the pan. Let cool slightly, and add enough egg to hold the mixture together. Chop the pecans, reserving 8, and add to the stuffing.

4. Using a teaspoon, fill the pocket in each chicken breast with some of the stuffing.

5. Melt another tablespoon of the butter in a flameproof casserole, and add the chicken breasts, skin-side down first. Brown over moderate heat, and turn over. Brown the other side quickly to seal.

6. Pour in the stock, cover the casserole, and cook for about 25-30 minutes in a preheated 350°F oven until tender.

7. When chicken is cooked, remove it to a serving plate to keep warm. Reserve and strain the cooking liquid.

8. Melt the remaining butter in a small saucepan, and stir in the flour. Cook to a pale straw color. Stir in the cooking liquid, and add the sherry. Bring to a boil and stir constantly until thickened. Add the reserved pecans and seasoning.

9. Spoon some of the sauce over the chicken. Garnish with chopped parsley or a bunch of watercress.

Step 1 Use a small, sharp knife to cut a pocket in each chicken breast.

Step 4 Open each pocket in the chicken, and spoon in the stuffing.

Cook's Notes

Time
Preparation takes about 30 minutes, cooking takes about 40 minutes

Variation
If pecans are unavailable, use hazelnuts. Crush the hazelnuts roughly for the garnish, and brown lightly in the butter before adding flour for the sauce.

Serving Idea
Serve with rice or sauté potatoes, broccoli and carrots.

SERVES 4-6

CHICKEN WITH EGGPLANT AND HAM STUFFING

Eggplants and ham make an unusual
stuffing, and add interest to roast chicken.

1 small eggplant
2 tablespoons butter or margarine
1 small onion, finely chopped
¾ cup chopped ham
2 cups fresh bread crumbs
2 teaspoons chopped mixed fresh herbs
1-2 eggs, beaten
Salt and freshly ground black pepper
1 3-pound roasting chicken
2 tablespoons additional butter, softened

Step 1 Sprinkle the cut surface of the eggplant lightly with salt, and let sit.

1. Cut the eggplant in half lengthwise and remove stem. Lightly score the surface with a sharp knife, and sprinkle with salt. Let sit for about 30 minutes for the salt to draw out any bitter juices.

2. Melt the butter in a medium saucepan, and when foaming, add the onion. Cook slowly to soften slightly.

3. Rinse the eggplant and pat dry. Cut into ½-inch cubes. Cook with the onion until fairly soft. Add the remaining ingredients, except the chicken and softened butter, beating in the egg gradually until the mixture just holds together. Add salt and pepper to taste.

4. Remove the fat from just inside the chicken cavity. Fill the neck end with the stuffing. Place any extra in a greased casserole. Tie the legs together, and place the chicken in a roasting pan. Spread over the softened butter, and roast in a preheated 350°F oven for about 1 hour, or until the juices from the chicken run clear when the thickest part of the thigh is pierced with a sharp knife.

5. Cook extra stuffing, covered, for the last 35 minutes of cooking time. Let the chicken sit for 10 minutes before carving. If wished, make a sauce with the pan juices.

Step 4 Remove the fat from just inside the cavity opening.

Cook's Notes

 Time
Preparation takes about 30 minutes, cooking takes about 5-6 minutes for the stuffing and about 1 hour for the chicken.

Variation
Other ingredients, such as chopped red or green bell peppers, celery or scallions, may be added to the stuffing.

Watchpoint
Do not stuff the chicken until ready to cook.

SERVES 4

CHICKEN THIGHS IN PERNOD

Your guests will feel extremely pampered
when they sit down to this dish.

2 tablespoons butter
8 chicken thighs
2 shallots, finely chopped
2 tablespoons water
5 tablespoons Pernod
Salt and freshly ground black pepper

Step 1 Sauté the chicken for 8 minutes to brown on all sides.

1. Melt the butter in a large skillet. When hot, sauté the thighs for 8 minutes, browning on all sides. Reduce the heat, add the shallots and water, and cover the skillet.

2. Simmer for 30-35 minutes longer, or until the chicken portions are cooked.

3. Increase the heat, and pour in the Pernod.

4. Set alight with a match, shake the skillet, and turn off the heat. When the flames die down, scrape up any browned juices from the bottom of the skillet.

5. Remove the chicken portions to a warm serving dish. Season the remaining juices with salt and pepper, and bring to a boil. Spoon over the chicken, and serve.

Step 3 Increase the heat, and pour in the Pernod.

Step 4 Scrape up any browned meat juices from the bottom of the skillet.

Cook's Notes

Time
Preparation takes about 20 minutes, cooking takes about 30-35 minutes.

Serving Idea
Serve on a bed of rice with a selection of seasonal vegetables.

Variation
Add a little cream to the sauce just before serving, and heat through.

SERVES 4

POUSSINS ESPAGNOLE

The olive oil in this recipe gives
a wonderful flavor to the sauce.

4 single (small) poussins
Salt and freshly ground black pepper
Olive oil, to brush
4 small wedges of lime or lemon
4 bay leaves
2 tablespoons olive oil
1 small onion, thinly sliced
1 clove garlic, crushed
1 pound tomatoes
⅔ cup red wine
⅔ cup chicken or vegetable stock
1 tablespoon tomato paste
1 green chili, seeded and thinly sliced
1 small red bell pepper, cut into thin strips
1 small green bell pepper, cut into thin strips
2 tablespoons chopped, blanched almonds
1 tablespoons pine nuts
12 small black olives, pitted
1 tablespoon raisins

1. Rub the poussins inside and out with salt and pepper. Brush the skins with olive oil, and push a wedge of lemon or lime, and a bay leaf into the cavity of each one.

2. Roast the poussins, uncovered, in a preheated 375°F oven for 45 minutes, or until just tender.

3. Meanwhile, heat the 2 tablespoons of olive oil in a large skillet, and cook the onion and the garlic over a low heat until they are soft, but not colored.

4. Cut a slit into the skins of each tomato, and plunge into boiling water for 30 seconds.

5. Using a sharp knife, carefully peel away the skins from the blanched tomatoes.

6. Chop the tomatoes roughly. Remove and discard the seeds and cores.

7. Add the chopped tomatoes to the cooked onion and garlic, and fry slowly for 2 minutes longer.

8. Add the remaining ingredients, and simmer for 10-15 minutes, or until the tomatoes have completely softened and the sauce has thickened slightly.

9. Arrange the poussins on a serving dish, and spoon a little of the sauce over each one.

10. Serve hot with the remaining sauce in a separate jug.

Step 3 Fry the onion and garlic slowly in the olive oil until they are soft but not colored.

Step 5 Using a sharp knife, carefully peel away the loosened skins from the blanched tomatoes.

Cook's Notes

Time
Preparation takes 15 minutes, cooking takes about 1 hour.

Serving Idea
Serve with rice and a mixed green salad.

Cook's Tip
If the poussins start to get too brown during the cooking time, cover them with foil.

Index